A
Hl
THE CHURCH OF ENGLAND

A POPULAR HISTORY OF THE CHURCH OF ENGLAND

BY
G. R. BALLEINE, M.A.

BROUGHT UP TO DATE BY
CANON G. C. B. DAVIES, D.D.

VINE BOOKS LTD.
7 WINE OFFICE COURT
LONDON EC4A 3DA

© G. R. BALLEINE, M.A.

First Published	.	.	.	1913
Second Impression	.	.	.	1914
Third Impression	.	.	.	1923
Fourth Impression	.	.	.	1938
Fifth Impression	.	.	.	1948
Sixth Impression	.	.	.	1954
Seventh Impression	.	.	.	1958
Eighth Impression	.	.	.	1961
Ninth Impression	.	.	.	1976
Revised Edition	.	.	.	1976

Made and printed in Great Britain by
Stanley L. Hunt (Printers) Ltd, Midland Road, Rushden, Northants

Foreword

"CHURCH History is dry stuff. No one but a fossil could take any interest in Canons of Cloveshoo or Constitutions of Clarendon or even in the Advertisements of Elizabeth. I would as soon sit down to study a work on Conic Sections." So scoffed my friend the Churchwarden. Yet he is a man who is fond of reading and keenly interested in his Church. And there are many who would agree with him. This book is written with the hope of helping some of them to see that they are suffering from a most extraordinary delusion. The religious development of a great nation, and that nation our own, must be a subject of absorbing interest, if we can approach it from the right point of view.

How shall we approach it? Some Church Histories have been written from the standpoint of an Archbishop's Commissary. They deal with Kings and Councils and Conferences, with the business of Bishops and Archdeacons. They move in an atmosphere immensely remote from anything that the average Churchman ever comes in touch with. But the present book deals with the Church as it is seen by the man in the pew, not by the man in the mitre. It keeps a typical English parish in the centre of the stage. It tries to trace the religion and worship of an ordinary village congregation through the different centuries. It aims at showing how the things with which every Churchman is familiar, gradually grew to be what they are today. It does not ignore what Bishops and Kings were doing at headquarters, but it studies these matters, not through the debates of the Council Chamber, but through the results which followed in the actual life of the parishes.

It is hardly necessary to add that Durford and its daughter parish Monksland are purely imaginary places, and so their vicars, squires, and villagers have never lived in the flesh; but they are typical of men and women who were very much alive in hundreds of actual villages, and every event placed in Durford did literally happen somewhere exactly as related. Even the Churchwardens' Accounts are authentic, though borrowed from other parishes. On the other hand every name and date connected with the world outside our two fictitious villages is sober, scientific history, into which no touch of fancy has been allowed to stray.

If this little book helps one reader to feel the fascination of the story of how God's labourers have toiled through some sixteen centuries to plough this stubborn English soil, so that the seeds of Truth may get a chance to grow; if it moves one reader to bestir himself and put his hand to the plough, the writer will be satisfied.

Preface

Some may question the re-issue, unaltered except for a final chapter, of a book which was first published in 1913. But immense changes during the past half century, bringing renewed talk of dis-establishment, have focussed attention again on the Church's relation with the State, so putting the subject of Church history back in perspective. If Church and State grew up together, the British people developing their laws and customs on religious principles, then Church history recounts the tangled paths of interaction, in which from time to time Churchmen influenced political affairs and statesmen guided Church reform.

By taking two imaginary villages, Durford and Monksland, and tracing the effect of religious movements on their two communities, Balleine has produced in popular form with fictional characters, the story of the Church's work in rural England until the end of the first World War. While national landmarks have their place, the author's viewpoint is that he "deals with the Church as it is seen by the man in the pew, not by the man in the mitre". The parish church, its religion and worship, are at the centre of the stage. Yet he incorporates genuine national events, and even material from churchwardens' accounts. "Continuity through change" is the keynote, with the hope that all who read, whether committed Churchmen or not, will feel themselves involved in a story. Here is the continuing record of the Church's work and witness in this land, to which we are all called, in however small a way, to play our part in practical commitment to Him who brought good news of great joy to the whole world.

Worcester,
May, 1976. COLLISS DAVIES.

Contents

Chapter	Page
1. How the Gospel came to Durford and was Driven Out	11
2. How the Church of England came into Being	19
3. How Men Tried to Flee from the World and how the World followed Them	28
4. How the Bishop of Rome gained supreme power in England	41
5. How Men Tried to reform the Church from Within and Without	54
6. How Durford's Sixth Church was built and used	74
7. How the Church of England got rid of the Pope, the Monks and much Superstition	90
8. How the Reformation was at last Victorious	103
9. How the Church of England had to Fight for its life against Rome and Geneva	119
10. How Geneva gained the Mastery	137
11. How Geneva lost its opportunity and Rome was finally Defeated	153
12. How the Church went to Sleep	168
13. How the Church Awoke from Slumber	175
14. How the Church enlarged its Vision	194

List of Illustrations

	Page
Map of the Seven Kingdoms	24
Shrine of St. Alban	38
Anglo-Saxon Church at Bradford-on-Avon	39
Administering Extreme Unction	63
John Wyclif	65
Grouped Lancet Lights	75
Decorated Window	76
Perpendicular Window, York Minster	78
Plan of Durford Church	79
A Mediaeval Confirmation	87
Caricature of a Monk	98
Destruction of Communion Rails	149

CHAPTER I

How the Gospel came to Durford and was driven out

WE are going to study together the story of the Church of England. To do so let us fix our eyes on the Kentish village of Durford. True, there is no such place on the map, in Kent or any other county; but we will take a typical village, and call it by that name; and as we watch the changes which come to one little church and parish, we shall gain some idea of what is happening through the country as a whole; for, until the nineteenth century crowded us into cities, the great majority of Englishmen have always lived in villages.

British Paganism

On a dark spring afternoon, somewhere between the year 29 and the year 33, the Son of God died on the Cross for the sins of the whole world, but Durford, three thousand miles away, knew nothing of that. It was only a group of wattled huts, fenced in with an earthen wall, buried in the depths of a great forest. Its tall, yellow-haired inhabitants, Maelgwn, Anllech, and their kin, worshipped a hundred obscure deities, gods of the streams and hills and forests, and the memory of the cruel rites with which they tried to woo them, still lingers in the local superstitions. Even in the present year of grace the boldest of the village hoydens will not dare to cross the stepping-stones on Midsummer Day, because the Dur is held on that day to be craving for a victim; but she does not know that her fear dates back to those old heathen times, when the white-robed Druid came to the village every Midsummer Day, and drowned a maiden as a sacrifice to the Spirit of the Brook. For the Celtic race even in those days was passionately religious, and Maelgwn and Anllech saw gods lurking in the simplest things around them. If a spring gushed up in the forest, if the waters of a stream began to fail, if a tree grew larger than its fellows, if a boar defied the huntsmen, assuredly a god was there, a god who was calling for sacrifice, and the best of all sacrifices was a man. Human victims dangled from the branches of every sacred tree. Human flesh was mingled with the corn before it was sown. And, if the lesser gods required this, how much more did the great ones, Belenos, the sun-god, Badbaatha, the war-goddess of victory, who was worshipped by the impaling of women. Every prisoner taken in war was always offered in sacrifice. When this supply failed, victims were drawn from the aged and the children and the women. Sometimes in an hour of great emergency the chief himself was sacrificed. At certain seasons there were horrible orgies of religious cannibalism, when the villagers feasted on the flesh of the victims they had slain. Such was the religion of Durford as our story opens, a religion of darkness, a religion of terror, a religion of blood.

The Coming of the Romans

Ten years later (A.D. 43) an event occurred which changed the whole current of our country's life. An army of 50,000 men came marching up the rough track which led from Durford to the sea. The Romans had arrived[1] to make Britain a province of their worldwide empire. They brought with them peace and justice and civilisation. Human sacrifice was now forbidden. Roads were made, bridges built, law courts established. Merchants, soldiers, and civil officials moved ever backward and forward, keeping the village in constant touch with the world across the sea. Maelgwn and Anllech began to wear togas and to talk bad Latin. But the Gospel did not yet reach our distant island. The old Paganism became less cruel, but

[1] Julius Caesar's raid ninety years before had left no permanent results.

it retained its power. Some of the people added to it the worship of the gods of Rome. Altars to Mars and Jupiter and Neptune began to make their appearance. But another hundred and fifty years had to pass away before we find any trace of Christianity in Britain.

The Coming of the Gospel

How did the True Faith come to Durford? No one can say. Was it that some legionary, who had learned the Truth in Italy, married one of our village girls and settled in the place? Was the builder of that Roman villa, whose tessellated floor can still be seen in the vicarage garden, a well-to-do Christian from Gaul, who had fled here to escape the persecution which was raging in Lyons and Vienne? Was it that some merchant travelled south with dusky British pearls, and there found the Pearl of Great Price? In these and a hundred other ways Christianity began to filter into the country. The seed took root and sprang up secretly, we know not how. All that we do know is that, by the beginning of the third century, Christians in distant lands – Tertullian in Africa, for example (A.D. 208), and Origen in Asia (A.D. 239) – write of the Church in Britain as already in existence. Many a village like Durford by this time had its little wattled church, and though large numbers of the people still remained pagan, and built the altars which we dig up sometimes dedicated "To the Old Gods", the more intelligent and open-minded were rapidly being won to the Faith.

Public Worship

Let us visit Durford Church one Sunday morning. It is sunrise, and all the Christians in the village have assembled for public worship. Two priests stand at the Lord's Table, for the British Church allows no one but a bishop to administer the Communion alone. They wear no special vestments; their dress is exactly the same as that of the laymen around.[1] They are married men, earning their living on weekdays as carpenters or masons; but they have each been duly ordained by a bishop. The service is in Latin, a language which all can understand. The preliminary service for the catechumens[2] has just ended, and all who are not full members of the Church are bidden to withdraw. The unbaptized, the children, the excommunicated quietly file out, and the Liturgy of the Faithful, the Communion Service begins. We notice several strange customs – the ceremonial combing of the priests' hair, the kiss of peace which all Church members have to give one another, but there are no non-communicants; the laity receive the Cup as well as the Consecrated Bread; the ritual which in later years grew up around the Mass has hardly yet begun to obscure and complicate the rite.

Persecution

But Christianity was still a forbidden religion, and soon there came a rough reminder of the fact. On the Feast of the God of Boundaries, A.D. 303, an appropriate day for putting an end to the Christian superstition, Diocletian the Emperor issued an edict that all churches were to be demolished, all copies of the Scriptures burnt, and all Christians outlawed. Britain was an outlying province, and Constantine the Governor not unfriendly, and so the persecution here was milder than abroad, but Durford Church was levelled to the ground, like all the other churches, and soon news came that the first British martyr had laid down his life for Christ. In every Christian home

[1] The first outward mark distinguishing clergy from laity was the tonsure, i.e., the shaving of the front of the head up to a line drawn from ear to ear. This was the badge of slavery, and was adopted by the clergy as a sign that they were bondservants of Christ. The practice began about the beginning of the sixth century. A special vestment for use in Church was not introduced till the seventh century, and then only through the clergy retaining for their ministrations the old-fashioned, flowing, secular robes, which were going out of use in ordinary daily life.

[2] I.e., those who are being prepared for baptism.

the story was repeated how Alban of Verulam, while still a pagan, hid a fugitive priest; how, as he watched his guest's behaviour, he too became a Christian; how he put on the priest's cloak and gave himself up in his stead; how, when ordered to sacrifice or die, he joyfully chose death; and, when he and his guards could not cross the bridge for the crowd of spectators, waded through the water, so eager was he to gain the martyr's crown.

The Councils

This was almost the last attempt of Roman Paganism to stamp out Christianity. In 313 the Emperor Constantine himself became a Christian, and the edict of Milan gave freedom of religion to every province of the Empire. Many who had fallen from the faith in the hour of persecution now asked to be re-admitted to the Church. What should be done with them? To decide this a Council was called at Arles (A.D. 314), and at this three British bishops were present. British bishops attended later a Council at Rimini (A.D. 359). And this is important, because it shows that all Western Christendom recognized the British Church as orthodox and duly organized. Her bishops were summoned as a matter of course to the greatest councils, and met the bishops of other countries on perfectly equal terms.

The Withdrawal of the Legions

For three hundred and sixty years Britain had been part and parcel of the Roman Empire, but now Durford began to see a strange and ominous sight. First one legion, and then another, marched down the village street on its way to the sea, and no fresh ones ever came to take their place. The Mistress of the world was fighting at home for her very life. Alaric and his Goths were pouring into Italy, and Rome had no troops to spare to defend her distant colonies. In 407 the last legion set sail, and Britain was left to protect herself as best she could.

Pelagianism

While the civil officials were grappling with the difficulties of the new position, the Church was troubled with the heresy of the Pelagians, whose "vain talk" is still denounced in our Thirty-Nine Articles. Pelagius was himself a Briton, "a big, fat dog from Albion, bloated with Scotch porridge," St. Jerome calls him in an indignant letter. Like many heretics he was a good man, but he believed that man could be good without the grace of God: whereas the Church has always taught that "we have no power to do good works pleasant and acceptable to God without the grace of God preventing us (i.e., first putting the thought into our minds), and working with us, when we have that good will". Pelagius taught his heresy in Rome and Carthage and the East, but there came to Durford the priest Agricola, whom Pelagius had sent to spread his views in Britain. Here, as elsewhere, he met with a mixed reception. Some of the richer folk inclined to the new doctrines, but the clergy and the poorer people stood fast for the old Faith.

Visit of Germanus

During the next twenty years the Pelagian views distinctly gained ground. But one day there arrived in the village (A.D. 429) a tall and dignified stranger, Germanus, Bishop of Auxerre one of the greatest orators of the age. The British bishops had invited him over to help them to check the heresy. He preached in church, and then went out, and preached in the open air, and, as a Breton by birth, he was able to speak to the people in the British tongue. With his companion the Bishop of Troyes, he passed from village to village, and soon the Pelagian leaders felt their followers slipping from them. They challenged the bishops to a public debate in the city of Verulam, but that was their undoing. When the day came, they spoke first, and then Germanus answered in such a flood of oratory, that the multitudes who had flocked to listen were won to his side in a moment, and his chief difficulty was not to convince them of the danger of heresy, but to prevent their tearing the Pelagian speakers to pieces.

The Coming of the Pirates

This is the last glimpse we get of the British Church in this part of England. For suddenly a far more serious problem arose. The question was no longer whether orthodox views on the Doctrine of Grace should prevail, but whether there should be a Christian Church at all in Britain. Even before the Romans withdrew, two sets of marauders had been giving trouble. The Picts, or painted folk, of Scotland were ever swarming over the wall, and having to be driven back; while savage pirates from Denmark and North Germany were constantly raiding the coast. When the legions left, these raids naturally increased in frequency: and at last the Government in despair adopted the fatal policy of trying to hire the pirates to repel the Picts. In 449 the rulers of Kent hired sea-rovers from Jutland. Then the inevitable dispute arose over pay or rations. The pirates turned on their employers: and the men of Durford watched from the forest tall mail-clad savages burning their church and homes, and putting their kinsmen to death. In a few years the Jutes had conquered the whole county; large numbers of the Christian inhabitants had been slain; those who remained were either outlaws hiding in the forests, or slaves kept by the conquerors to till the ground. Northward in Essex, westward in Sussex, bands of Saxon sea-robbers did the same thing. Further north the Angles were winning all the East coast. More Saxons seized the district which they named Wessex. By 580 half Britain had passed into possession of the pirates, and in that half all outward observance of the Christian Faith had been stamped out in fire and blood.

English Paganism

Let us watch what happened at Durford. The village

had been burnt to the ground in the first raid. When the time came to divide the land, this district fell to the Glaestings, a group of ten families, who were all kinsmen. Their first act was to remove all trace of the British village, lest spells and enchantments should haunt the stones and walls. Ten homesteads were then built with wood from the neighbouring forest. Huts were thrown up around them in which the slaves could sleep, and the whole was surrounded with an earthen rampart, topped with a quickset hedge. Herethryth and Waerlaf, Ceolmund and Hwita were now the chief men of the village, fierce heathen, worshipping those German gods whose names we still repeat when we call the days of our week Tiw's day and Woden's day, Thor's day and Frig's day. And of these Greater Gods Woden was King. Minor deities might be appeased with offerings of dogs and hawks, but Woden would accept no lesser sacrifice than a man. The temple of Woden with its sacred stump stood on the site of the Christian church, and on certain days of the year great feasts were held around it; but the average man was far more influenced by the terrorism of the lesser gods, the ghosts who dwelt in solitary places and stalked through the land at night, the goblins who haunted the sacred circles of the old religion, the valkyrs and the nicors, the imps and demons, the werwolves, the nightmares and the elves, the prolific host of Grendel the Evil One, against which it was necessary to defend oneself by carefully woven chains of charms and spells and incantations. Totemism or animal worship was also practised, and in Kent the White Horse was specially sacred. The Christian slaves, no doubt, clung to their religion in secret, but they were ignorant and crushed with suffering; their leaders had fled to the West or over the sea to Brittany; there was no public worship and no means of instruction. What wonder, if their faith grew feeble as the years passed by! For a century and a half Durford was once more a heathen village.

Chapter 2

How the Church of England came into being

Bertha, Queen of Kent

YEARS passed on, and we see the fourth generation of the Glaestings. Durford had become a prosperous village. The great-grandchildren of the pirates had settled down as farmers, and one of their number – let us call him Wulfric – was now thegn or squire. It was his duty to call out the warriors and to administer justice, and three times a year he rode to the King's Court in Canterbury. Here once more it was possible to see, if he desired to do so, a Christian service celebrated in a Christian church. For years the old British Church of St. Martin had been standing ruined and roofless, but now Ethelbert, King of Kent, had married a Christian lady, and Queen Bertha, daughter of the King of Paris, had brought to her new home a bishop named Luidhard, and the King had restored the old church and given it her to worship in. Soon some of the men of Kent began to wish to learn more of the Queen's religion, and letters were written to the bishops of Gaul asking them to send teachers. But the worldly and corrupt Frankish Church had neither will nor power to undertake a mission. So the Temple of Woden still stood in the centre of Durford village, with its holy ring, on which oaths were sworn, and its bloodstone, where the victims were sacrificed, and its wrinkled hag, who practised witchcraft, and raised the spirits of the dead.

The Coming of Augustine

But one day (597) strangers from Rome landed in the Isle of Thanet, declaring that they had a message for the King, which, if he would receive it, would enable him to gain an everlasting kingdom. And Ethelbert called his thegns around him, and crossed to the Island to meet them. As Wulfric stood behind his King under the oak at Ebbe's Fleet, he saw forty Italian monks in their russet robes slowly marching two by two behind a silver cross. He heard the strange rise and fall of the Gregorian chant. He saw a Face, painted on wood, borne like a banner in the midst, that grave Byzantine Face of Christ which we see in ancient mosaics. He saw the tall figure of Augustine towering above his fellows, and he heard him preach in the Latin tongue, which the Frankish interpreters did their best to translate, as he told "how the tender-hearted Jesus redeemed the world by His throes, and opened the Kingdom of Heaven to all believers". And Wulfric listened with eager interest to his King's reply: "Beautiful indeed are the promises ye bring, but they are new and unproven. I cannot forsake the faith of my fathers which I have held so long. But since ye have come from a far country to make known things which ye deem to be true, we welcome you with friendly hospitality; we will provide for your needs; nor do we forbid you to preach your religion and win whom ye can."

Baptism of Ethelbert

It is only later that Wulfric and his friends would have heard the story of why these monks left their monastery on the Coelian Hill, of the English slave-boys – not Angles but angels – whom Gregory, their bishop, had seen in the Forum at Rome, and of the great desire that had seized his heart to win their kin for Christ. But there would be much to talk of when they returned to Durford, and more when they learned how the King had given the monks a house in Canterbury, how they were preaching daily in the Church of St. Martin, and how many of the English were forsaking the gods and coming to them for baptism. Then the astounding tidings came that Ethelbert himself, whom all men believed to be of the house and lineage of Woden, had declared that he too would serve the White Christ, and at the font had been admitted into the circle of his followers; and that Augustine, the tall monk, had set sail for Gaul to be consecrated as Archbishop of the English race.

The Conversion of Kent

In Durford, Wulfric summoned the Gemot or parish council, and all the freemen met to decide on their course of action. The King had declared that he would compel no man to become a Christian. The Keeper of the Temple no doubt worked hard with her sorceries and spells; and Kentish men have never been wont to make up their minds hastily. But, by the time Augustine returned, they had come to their decision. The old feeling of tribal loyalty had prevailed. It was impossible for King and People to serve different gods. Where the King led the way, his People must always follow. In scores of villages the same logic led to the same determination, and on Christmas Day more than ten thousand persons were publicly baptized by Augustine in the River Swale.

The Hallowing of Heathenism

What difference did this make to Durford? Less than might be imagined. Gregory had given the missionaries instructions to make as few changes as possible in the customs of the people. Even the heathen festivals were to be retained and Christianized. Thus the Teutonic High Festival at the beginning of winter was christened Martinmas, and the geese were still slain and eaten, but now in honour of St. Martin. The mid-winter Yule revelries, with the burning of the Yule log and the killing of the Yule boar, and the hanging up of the mistletoe bough in memory of Baldur the Beautiful, were boldly claimed as rejoicings over the birth of Christ. The spring feast of the Goddess Eostre with her Easter eggs became the Festival of the Resurrection. Rogation Days were merely the continuance of the mid-May heathen processions, and the leaping through bonfires on Midsummer Eve was retained to the glory of St. John the Baptist. Even the most sacred symbol of all, the mighty hammer of Thor, needed but little alteration, and it became a cross.

Church Building

The wooden temple of Woden was, however, pulled down, and with much sprinkling of holy water the temple enclosure was consecrated to the service of Christ. On the south side a large stone cross was erected, and every Sunday one of the Canterbury monks rode over and preached to the people from its steps. Beneath its shadow he used to place his portable altar, a small piece of wood covered with silver, and there celebrated Mass in the open air. Later he felt that a permanent altar would be more seemly and convenient, and he built a small chapel or chancel to protect it from the rain, leaving one side perfectly open that all might see and hear. Then it began to dawn on the people that the climate of Kent was not at all times suited for outdoor worship, and for their own comfort and protection they built a nave in front of the priest's chapel, and from that day to this the parishioners have had to keep the nave in repair, and the Rector has had to repair his own chancel. In this way Durford obtained its third church, a small oblong building with no architectural beauty, with rubble walls and thatched roof, and no windows on the north side for fear the devil should peep in, its only glory an awe-inspiring picture of the Doom with which a Canterbury artist had covered the western wall.

Augustine and the British Bishops

All Kent was now nominally Christian, but Augustine's work was not yet accomplished. Two tasks remained: to get in touch with the British Church which still survived in the West; and to get in touch with the other heathen kingdoms. By the help of Ethelbert he arranged a meeting with the British bishops. For a century and a half the British Church had been cut off from the Continent by the solid wedge of Anglo-Saxon heathenism, with the result that its customs varied from those of other Churches. For example, the Roman Church had revised its way of calculating the date of Easter, but the British Church still used the old tables. British priests shaved the front of their heads, while Romans shaved the crown. In Baptisms also there was some point of difference; the Romans plunged the child three times beneath the water, and possibly the British use was only to immerse it once. These were small matters, but they needed adjustment, if the Christian Church was to show a united front to Paganism. Seven British bishops came to meet Augustine, and with them monks and scholars from the Abbey of Bangor by the Dee, but first they consulted a wise and holy hermit. His answer was: "Our Lord saith, Take My yoke, for I am meek and lowly. If this Augustine is meek and lowly, know that he bears Christ's yoke. But, if he is harsh and proud, regard not his teaching." "How can we tell this?" they asked. "Contrive," the hermit answered, "that he shall come first to the place of meeting. If he rises to receive you, know that he is a servant of Christ. But if he despise you, and will not rise, let him be despised by you." This was no mere matter of courtesy, but a vital question: Would Augustine receive them as equals or as inferiors? But the Archbishop was armed with a letter from the Pope in which it was written: "The bishops of Britain we entrust to you. Teach the ignorant. Strengthen the weak. Correct those that are perverse," and, when the visitors arrived, he retained his seat, like a Prince receiving a humble deputation of his subjects, and the bishops replied, that they declined to give up their old customs and refused to recognize him as their Archbishop. All hope of union with the ancient Church of the land was at an end.

The other Kingdoms

There remained the six kingdoms of the English which

were still heathen – Northumbria, Mercia, East Anglia, Essex, Sussex, Wessex – and to these the missionaries now turned their attention. Essex was one of the states which owned Ethelbert as overlord, and by his influence the King was baptized (604), and Mellitus, one of Augustine's monks, consecrated as Bishop of London. A few years later Raedwald of East Anglia, another vassal king, consented to be christened. Later still (626) Edwin of Northumbria, who had married Ethelbert's daughter, also became a Christian; the Northumbrian Witan in solemn assembly accepted Christianity; the heathen temples were destroyed; and Paulinus, another of the Italian monks, became Bishop of the Northumbrians. But all these promising beginnings were doomed to end in failure. Raedwald soon relapsed into heathenism, though he retained an altar of Christ in the temple of his idol. The men of Essex drove out their bishop, as soon as the king died (616). Edwin of Northumbria was slain in battle (633) by the heathen Mercians, and Paulinus fled back South, and became Bishop of Rochester. The sole result of Augustine's mission was the conversion of Kent.

How were the other kingdoms eventually won? In various ways. Wessex was converted by Birinus, a freelance missionary from North Italy (634). Felix, a bishop from Burgundy, won (636) East Anglia for the Faith. The three largest kingdoms were evangelized by Irish monks. The Church of Ireland was a sister of the British Church. It had grown up entirely apart from the influence of Rome, and it stood at this time without a rival in its love of learning, its passion for holiness and its resistless energy. It had made its own country an island of saints, and now was flinging itself into battle with heathenism abroad. Columban had carried the Gospel to Burgundy, St. Gall to Switzerland, and Columba had built (563) a monastery in the Island of Iona from which he could work among the Picts of Scotland. From this monastery (635) came Aidan and a party of monks to the Island of Lindisfarne off the coast of Northumbria: and from Lindisfarne they began those mission journeys, which won back the northern kingdom for Christ; they pressed on and evangelized the whole of heathen Mercia; they sent out Cedd, who reconverted the apostate kingdom of Essex. By 660 all England was nominally Christian, except the little kingdom of Sussex, shut in between the forest and the sea.

The Whitby Conference

But there was no such thing yet as a Church of England. There were seven Churches in the country. The Church of Kent and the Church of Northumbria; the Church of Mercia and the Church of the East Angles; the Church of the East Saxons and the Church of the West Saxons; and the British Church. And these Churches were divided one from the other by those very points of difference which Augustine had discussed with the British bishops; for the Churches taught by Irish monks agreed with the Britons, while those taught by missionaries from the Continent agreed with Augustine; and it sometimes happened that Canterbury kept Easter a whole month later than London.

In 664 the King of Northumbria brought the matter to a head, when he found that he would be celebrating Easter on the day on which his Kentish-trained Queen would be keeping Palm Sunday, and he called a Conference at Whitby to discuss the question. Most of those present were attached to the old system, but there was an eager minority on the other side, led by Wilfrid, Abbot of Ripon, a young Northumbrian, who had visited Rome, and returned an enthusiast for all things Roman. Many learned arguments were brought forward, astronomical, theological, historical, but, as is so often the case with a primitive people, an utterly inconclusive point at last carried the day. Colman, the successor of Aidan at Lindisfarne, claimed the authority of St. John for the old system. Wilfrid promptly claimed for the new the authority of St. Peter, "to whom our Lord said, I give thee the keys of the Kingdom of Heaven". The King at once asked Colman the question, "Did our Lord speak thus to St. Peter?" and, when he answered "Yes", the King closed the discussion. "I dare not," he said, "decide against the door-keeper of Heaven, lest haply, when I come to the gates, He will not let me through". Henceforth Northumbria definitely adopted the continental custom, not only with regard to Easter, but also with regard to the other matters of dispute. Essex and Mercia soon followed its example. The six English kingdoms had now one uniform use, though the British Church stood aloof for more than a hundred years.[1]

Theodore of Tarsus

A strong leader was now needed to weld the six Churches into one, and much depended on the appointment to the vacant See of Canterbury. The English nominee died at Rome before his consecration, and the Pope selected in his place Theodore of Tarsus, an elderly layman of sixty-six, long past the age when it is easy to adapt oneself to new conditions, an Asiatic, unable to speak a single word of

[1] The North Welsh yielded in 768; the South Welsh in 777.

English. A more amazing choice can hardly be imagined, yet he proved himself exactly the man for the work. Instead of confining himself to Kent, as all his predecessors had done, he visited all the six kingdoms, and everywhere received a welcome as Archbishop of the English. He filled up vacant sees, divided dioceses, where they seemed too large, suppressed irregularities, and on 24 September, 673, presided at Hertford over the first national Synod of the English Church. Here it was agreed that no bishop should trespass into the diocese of another, that monks should not wander at will from monastery to monastery, that no priest should quit his diocese without letters dismissory, that the marriage and divorce laws of every diocese should be the same, and that a convocation of the whole Church should be held once a year at Cloveshoch, a place which we cannot now identify with certainty. The meeting of those five bishops and their clergy in that little East Saxon town marks an epoch in the history of our Church and nation. For the first time Angles and Saxons met for common consultation, but they met not as fellow-countrymen but as fellow-churchmen. Ignorant people sometimes assert that the Church was established by Parliament. But the fact is that long before there was any Parliament or any English nation, thanks to Theodore of Tarsus, there was one united Church of England, obeying one set of canons, acknowledging the authority of one archbishop, using the same prayers and ceremonies from the Firth of Forth to the English Channel. There were still seven Kingdoms, but only one Church. The Church of England is 150 years older than the State.

Chapter 3

How men tried to fly from the world and how the world followed them

Durford Minster

ENGLAND had been converted by monks. The English Church had been organized by monks. So monasteries played an important part in all its early history. Our picture will not be complete, unless we place a Minster (i.e., monastery) in Durford, not in the village itself, but in some quiet clearing in the woods, where Wulfric gave half a hide of land to his daughter Deorwyn. This was no great abbey to compare with those which the Kentish royal family had lately built and endowed – Christ Church and St. Peter and St. Paul at Canterbury, Lyminge Abbey, Dover Abbey, Folkestone Abbey, Reculver Abbey, the minster in Sheppey and the minster in Thanet – but it was typical of the small foundations built by large land-owners as a refuge for a sister or a daughter. A stone church, lofty but not beautiful, for the English had at this time no skill in architecture. On the north side the men's quarters – a garden with a cloister round it, and round the cloister the cells, the chapter-house, the workshops, the refectory, and the kitchen. On the south side similar buildings for the mynchens or nuns; for a curious feature of early English monasticism was this, that men and women lived side by side under the rule of an Abbess. Outside, the fields which their labour had already begun to make fertile. Around all, a broad and silent belt of forest.

Monasticism was no new thing. Three hundred and fifty years before, Christians in Egypt had fled to the desert, and there drawn together in small communities.

The Rule of St. Benedict

From Egypt the practice spread to the West. The British Church had its monasteries, and the Irish Church consisted of little else. But, about half a century before the landing of Augustine, Benedict of Nursia had drawn up his famous Rule, which transformed all the monasteries that were in touch with Rome. Its chief aim was to check the craze for making "records" in austerities, which had been the main feature of the monasteries before him. In place of a wild individualism, in which every monk tried to outdo his brother, he introduced absolute obedience, even in self-mortification. "In a monastery the Abbot is considered to take the place of Christ." "In all that he commands the Abbot must be moderate, remembering the discretion of Jacob, when he said, 'If I cause my flocks to be overdriven, they will all perish'." For the old asceticism he substituted the discipline of continuous work. For the old solitude he substituted a life in which men lived, worked, and worshipped always with their fellows, holding all their property in common. "No one shall presume to keep as his own anything whatever; neither book, nor tablets, nor pen; nothing at all. All things are to be common to all." "The beds shall be frequently searched by the Abbot to guard against the vice of hoarding." Augustine's monastery on the Coelian Hill was probably Benedictine; certainly Wilfrid had learned the Rule during his travels on the Continent, and when the Irish customs were suppressed, the Rule of St. Benedict became the law in all English monasteries.

Monastic Life

Let us watch a summer day in Durford Minster. At 2 a.m. the monks are sleeping on their beds of straw, the Prior in the midst. Every man is fully dressed,[1] with his

---

[1] Anglo-Saxon monks seldom removed their clothes. St. Cuthbert did not take off his shoes from one Maunday Thursday to another, when the solemn foot-washing took place.

cowl drawn over his head. The Sacrist enters and awakens them. With bowed heads they glide through the cloisters to the church for Uhtsong. Here they remain for two hours chanting Psalms and Responses. Then comes a short break for relaxation, and at dawn they return to the church for Aftersong. Then they wash and have breakfast, and pass to the Chapter Meeting, where all the business of the house is done, and judgement passed on transgressors. Primesong at six is followed by work in the fields or forge or mill. Undersong at nine is followed by study in the cloister. Middaysong at noon is followed by dinner, rest, and recreation. Nonesong at two is followed by another spell of field labour. Evensong at six is followed by supper and the reading aloud of the lives of saints in the Chapterhouse. Then about half-past seven comes Nightsong, followed by silence and bed. The mynchens next door have been spending their time in much the same manner, but their services have been later than the monks, so that they have never met even in the church, and their work has taken the form of spinning and weaving and embroidery.

Some English Monks

These minsters trained a certain number of very noble Christians. There were brilliant scholars like Aldhelm of Malmesbury (d. 709), whose fame drew to his feet disciples from many distant lands, and Biscop (d. 690), the great collector of manuscripts, to whom men gave the name of Benedict, the blessed, and, greatest marvel of them all, the Venerable Bede. At a moment when learning had reached its lowest ebb in Western Europe, it is startling to find in a remote corner of barbarous Northumbria this monk of Jarrow (d. 735) writing his Church Histories and Commentaries on the Bible, noting the readings of various manuscripts, pointing out which are faulty, comparing the Vulgate and the older Latin version with the Greek, quoting copiously from Ambrose and Basil, Chrysostom and Jerome, Cyprian, Cyril and Augustine, drawing illustrations from Virgil and Ovid, Pliny and Plautus, Horace and Sallust and Cicero, revealing an amazing knowledge of the bypaths of theological controversy and of the doctrines of the obscurest heretics. Side by side with the scholars were simple-minded saints, men like Cuthbert (d. 687), who trudged through the dreary swamps of the Border district to teach the lonely country folk around their turf fires, and Caedmon, the neat-herd (c. 670), who became the father of English poetry. Here too were bred a race of heroic missionaries, the men and women who won Germany for the Christian faith: Willibrord of Ripon, who with twelve companions set out (690) to convert Frisia; Swidbert, who carried the Gospel to Prussia (693); Winfred (martyred 753), who evangelized Hesse and Thuringand won for himself the title of Boniface, the good-doer; Walburga (d. 779) and Lioba and the thirty nuns, who left Wimborne for the dark pine forests in the valley of the Tauber; and with these may be reckoned Alcuin (d. 800), the friend and adviser of Charlemagne. Throughout the whole of the eighth century the English minsters poured a steady stream of missionaries into Germany.

Seeds of Decay

The ideal of the monks was undoubtedly a most attractive one, and in certain cases it produced very fine results, but, taken as a whole, it did not work. The whole history of the system is a dreary succession of failures, followed by drastic reform, followed again by failure. And Anglo-Saxon monasteries in particular contained many points of weakness. One of these was the tendency to use them as reformatories. Every convicted adulteress was compelled to enter a convent. A thief might choose whether he would become a monk or a slave. Thus monasteries became filled with bad characters, and their tone deteriorated. Again, they were treated as benefices in the gift of the family of the founder, and an abbess, who was a saint, might be succeeded by a lady of very different temperament.

In the eighth century many monasteries became anything but homes of prayer. First we hear that monks and mynchens are dropping monastic dress. Aldhelm, who died in 709, described some nuns he had seen, with red shoes, scarlet tunics, and violet vests, their head-dress decked with gay ribbons hanging down to their ankles, their hair crisped with curling-tongs, and their nails pared like the talons of a falcon. And the dropping of the dress was only a sign of a general decay of discipline. The work in the fields, on which Benedict had laid so much emphasis, was now done by paid servants or by slaves. No longer did monks eat their food in silence, while one of the brethren read the Bible aloud from the pulpit. Meals were enlivened by the antics of buffoons and jesters. Visitors of both sexes wandered freely through the minsters. The Synod of Clovesho (747) complained that nuns were causing grave suspicion to fall on their Order by receiving and entertaining lay folk in their cells. Of one Abbot of St. Alban's we are told that his chief occupation was hunting, and that he "gave great scandal by the numbers of women he invited to dine in the Abbey, therein exceeding all bounds of decency"; while his successor, another famous sportsman, "wasted the goods of his church with players and scandalous persons". The letters of Boniface and Alcuin give the same impression, that drunkenness was terribly rife in the minsters, and other vices common.

The Coming of the Vikings

Upon a Church which tolerated this came down the scourge of God. For three centuries the tide of heathen invasions had ceased; but now through Denmark and its surrounding islands the rumour began to spread of English monasteries, rich and unprotected, of gold and silver, captives and cattle, to be had for the taking, of expeditions far more profitable than hunting the walrus or the whale; and pirate ships, manned by men who worshipped Thor and Woden, came rushing south, eager for plunder, just as the English themselves had done in days gone by. In 795 Aidan's monastery at Lindisfarne was sacked. Next summer the great Abbey at Wearmouth was burned to the ground. For fifty years every summer the Vikings came, sometimes to Northumbria, sometimes to the Fen Country, sometimes to Wessex, or to Cornwall, burning, harrying, murdering, tossing children on to their spears, carving blood eagles on the backs of priests; and in all the Churches a new petition was added to the Litany, "From the fury of the Northmen, good Lord, deliver us". In 850 the Vikings seized Thanet and destroyed the minster. They sailed up the Stour, and stormed Canterbury with great slaughter, and – ominous fact for the future – when winter came, they did not withdraw. First Thanet, then Sheppey, became permanent Danish settlements. Then in 865 all East Kent was ravaged. Durford would share the fate of the other villages. Nothing was left of church or minster but some blackened ruins. Parish priest and monks and mynchens all alike were slain. Thor and Woden had had their revenge.

Alfred

By this time the Vikings' aim was conquest, not plunder. In 867 Northumbria became a Danish kingdom. In 870 "the Host rode into East Anglia; the King they slew, and the whole land brought they under, and broke down all the minsters that ever they came to". In 874 Mercia was conquered. By 878 the only point of resistance left was the little Isle of Athelney in the Somerset marshes, where Alfred, King of the West Saxons, had taken refuge. But then the tide turned. Alfred's great victory at Ethandune freed Wessex and Kent. Guthrum and thirty of the Danish chiefs received baptism; and the Vikings settled down in the fifteen counties that remained in their hands, and before long became absorbed in the Christian population.

The Secular Canons

But by this time English monasticism was dead. The

wealth of the monasteries had caused them to bear the full brunt of the storm. The Danes had moved from minster to minster, plundering, murdering, burning, and though a few monks survived – at Crowland, for example, which had been one of the largest abbeys, five old men continued to live among the ruins – no fresh recruits could anywhere be found. When Alfred tried (888) to establish a monastery at Athelney, "he found," wrote Asser, his friend and chaplain, "not one noble or freeman, who would of his own accord submit to monastic life. The desire for this life had utterly died away among all the nation." Practically all the minster property that survived the storm passed into the hands of secular canons. Just as monks professed to follow the Rule of St. Benedict, so canons professed to follow a Rule drawn up about 750 by Chrodegang, Bishop of Metz. Like monks they were required to live and worship together, but there were many marked points of difference. Canons were clergy, whereas most monks were laymen. Canons were seculars, that is to say, they lived and worked in the world, whereas monks were supposed to have withdrawn from the world to the cloister. Monks were celibate, whereas in England, where the celibacy of the parochial clergy had not yet been enforced, many of the canons were married men. Monks held their property in common, but under the new system the monastic property was divided into prebends or portions, one of which was given to each canon. But it did not answer. In many cases all pretence of common life was abandoned, and the canons lived with their families on the prebendal farms, leaving the services in the abbey church to poorly paid substitutes. So deeply rooted had the abuse become, that when a Winchester reformer deprived the absentees of their canonries, and appointed in their place the men who were doing the duty, the new canons promptly engaged substitutes to sing the services for them, and disappeared to take possession of their new estates.

The Benedictine Revival

The sight of these rich, easy-going gentlemen appropriating to their private use the property of the Church, led men to forget the past failure of monasticism, and to desire its revival. In 945 Dunstan became Abbot of the ancient Minster of Glastonbury, which was then occupied by a few seculars. He soon restored the common life, and rebuilt the church, but did not yet venture to enforce the Benedictine Rule. Later (954) he sent Aethelwold his prior and some of his monks to Abingdon to revive an old minster there. But these were the only two monasteries with any kind of monastic life, and even in them the Rule of St. Benedict was not observed. Meanwhile the two abbots came in touch with monasticism abroad. Dunstan, exiled through a Court intrigue, took refuge in an Abbey in Ghent; Aethelwold sent one of his monks to Fleury, the abbey which contained the bones of St. Benedict, to study the methods there; and both were filled with a deep desire to revive in their own land the Benedictine system. Their chance came in 959, when Edgar the Peacewinner, great-grandson of Alfred, became sole king. "I, Edgar," he writes in one of his charters, "having been exalted by the grace of God to a height never enjoyed by any of my forefathers, have often considered what offering I should make to the King of Heaven, and Heavenly Love suddenly suggested to my mind that I should rebuild all the holy monasteries throughout my kingdom, which are not only visibly ruined with mouldering shingles and worm-eaten boards, but have become internally neglected and almost destitute of the worship of God. Wherefore, ejecting illiterate clerks, subject to the discipline of no regular order, I have appointed pastors of a holier race." Dunstan became Archbishop of Canterbury, Aethelwold, Bishop of Winchester, and Oswald, one of the monks of Fleury, Bishop of Worcester. Ruined abbeys were restored with astonishing rapidity. In five years the King himself rebuilt forty-seven. A more difficult task was to eject the seculars from monasteries which they had occupied, but though the struggle brought the kingdom to the verge of civil war, this was also accomplished in many cases. At Winchester, for example, Aethelwold summoned the canons to a service in the church, where they found a heap of cowls on the floor in front of the bishop's throne. All went smoothly till the verse came, "Serve the Lord with fear," when the bishop burst in with a voice of thunder, "Mean ye what ye sing? Will ye serve the Lord with fear? Then take up those cowls. I will have no hesitation. Put on that dress or go." "Whereupon three obeyed: the rest were thrust out from their canonries." Meanwhile a party of monks from Abingdon were peeping in at the door, waiting to take the place of those who should be expelled. By the end of the tenth century, though the seculars still remained in possession of some of the abbeys, the south and east of England were once more covered with monasteries.

The triumph of the monks was accompanied by a great outburst of superstition. Everywhere bones of saints were discovered, and worshipped with wild enthusiasm.

Relic Worship

"While there were Canons in the old Minster," wrote the Winchester chronicler, "St. Swithin wrought no miracle, but, when they were put out, wonders began and swarmed". "The burial ground," wrote another, "was so full of crippled folk, that people could hardly get into the Minster. Both walls were hung all round, from one end to the other, with crutches and stools of cripples who had been healed, and yet they could not put up half of them." When bones, supposed to be those of St. Aldhelm, were discovered at Malmesbury, soldiers had to be sent to keep order amongst the throngs of pilgrims. Monasteries hunted high and low for relics, and stooped to very dubious methods to obtain them. The Abbot of Ely (974) made the whole village of Dereham drunk, and then stole from the church the wonder-working bones of St. Werburga. Durham secured its most famous relics in a way even less commendable. Alfred of Westowe, "a priest whose works won for him the closest friendship of St. Cuthbert," served God by burglary. He visited all the churches of Northumbria, and by the story of a vision persuaded the clergy to allow him to adore their relics, and in almost every case he succeeded in appropriating a bone. But the prize on which he had set his heart was the body of the Venerable Bede, and at last (1020) after many failures he was successful, and the contents of the canvas bag, which he brought back from Jarrow, made Durham one of the greatest pilgrimage centres in the country.

The Relics of St. Alban

But the relics which drew the largest crowds were those of St. Alban. In 795 King Offa of Mercia had dreamed a dream, in consequence of which he caused an ancient barrow to be opened, and declared that the skeleton, that was found inside, was that of the first British martyr. Twelve other bones were found with it, and it was decided that these must be relics of the twelve Apostles, brought to England by Germanus, when he visited Verulam. These remains were regarded with the deepest reverence; but one day (874) they were seized by Vikings, and carried off to Denmark. Ergwin, one of the St. Alban's monks, followed them, and gained admission to the Danish monastery as a novice; after some years he returned, asserting that he had succeeded in stealing back the relics. The Danish monks, however, declared that Ergwin was a liar, and that the body was still in their possession. In 1042 there came a fresh threat of a Danish invasion, and the Abbot of St. Alban's sent a message to the Abbot of Ely, whose monastery was almost inaccessible in its marshes, asking him to guard the precious relics for him. When the danger was over, the monks of Ely sent back the shrine, but they placed in it a skeleton from their cemetery, keeping the reputed relics of the martyr for their own high altar. But the Abbot of St.

Shrine of St. Alban.

Alban's replied, that he had not been so simple-minded as to trust the Ely monks with the real relics; those had remained all the time hidden in his own Abbey, and Ely had stolen secular bones of no particular value. This story illustrates the doubtful authenticity of almost all these relics. The bones, which Offa dug up, were probably those of some pagan chieftain; and even of those bones no one could tell whether the real ones were in Denmark, Ely, or St. Albans; yet every year they drew thousands of pilgrims to each of the rival monasteries.[1] The belief in the power and sanctity of relics was practically universal.

[1] The offerings of the pilgrims proved a profitable source of income to the monasteries. We have no figures for these early years, but in the fourteenth century the gifts at the shrine of St. Cuthbert at Durham brought in, in modern money, an average of £750 a year; those at the shrine of St. Mary at Walsingham over £3,000 a year; those at the shrine of St. Thomas at Canterbury about £4,000.

Even level-headed men like Canute and Harold paid vast sums to obtain the bones of obscure Burgundian martyrs.

The Eleventh Century

Meanwhile the old England was dying in a welter of fire and blood. The treacherous massacre of the Danes on St. Brice's Day (1002); the arrival of Swegn Forkbeard to avenge his murdered sister; the pelting to death of Alphege, Archbishop of Canterbury, with ox-bones; Swegn, king for one year; Ethelred, king for another; then the red reign and poisoning of Edmund Ironside. Durford might well believe that the end of the world was at hand. In the village itself, when the Danes were absent, the routine of Church life went on as usual. Sunday would be spent in the orthodox way. "It is proper that every Christian should come on Saturday night to the church, bringing a light with him, and hear Vesper-Song, and after midnight Uhtsong, and come again with his offering in the morning to the Solemn Mass. After that, let him return home and regale himself with his neighbours, taking care that he commit no excess in eating or drinking." Sometimes a criminal would crash through the woods to claim sanctuary

Anglo-Saxon Church at Bradford-on Avon.

at the altar. Sometimes the village would be thrilled by an ordeal. Perhaps it was Waerlaf who swore that Waerstan had murdered Wulflaf the swine-herd. Waerstan on oath has declared that he is perfectly innocent. So Ailric the thegn must bring him to Mass three days running, and on the third day, before the service begins, the priest lays a bar of iron across a glowing brazier. At the last collect he takes it off with a pair of tongs, sprinkles it with holy water, and lays it on a stone, with a prayer to the God of Justice to reveal the truth. Then Waerstan must pick it up, and carry it three paces. The priest will then bandage his hand, and seal it with the Church seal. In three days' time the bandage will be removed, and then "if festering blood be found, he shall be judged guilty; but, if the burn be healed, praise shall be rendered to God". Meanwhile national affairs were drifting from bad to worse. For a time (1017-35) England was a province of Canute's great Northern Empire. Then came brief and bloody reigns of two Danish kings. Then the English Royal family was restored (1042) in the person of that most incompetent of saints, Edward the Confessor. The Church, like the nation, showed every sign of decay and exhaustion. Bishoprics fell into the hands of weak and unworthy men. Monks once more grew lazy and luxurious, parochial clergy only too often drunken and disreputable. In many a village the old Paganism began to lift up its head. Thor the Thunderer and Woden the Truthseeker had not been utterly forgotten; and, in spite of strongly worded laws for the suppression of deofolgilden or devils' guilds, men began to meet secretly for "heathenship by way of sacrifice and divinings". Still larger numbers lost all touch with any form of religion. A slow, stupid, swinish sensuality was sapping the nation's strength. Church and State alike required fresh blood and discipline, and they found both (1066) when Harold fell under the Dragon Banner, and William and his Norman adventurers became masters of England.

CHAPTER 4

How the Bishop of Rome gained supreme power in England

The Church and the Feudal System

DURFORD quickly felt the effect of the Norman Conquest. First came mourning for sons and fathers who had fallen with Harold. Then the Conqueror and his host arrived, marching from Dover to Canterbury. Then one day came Roger de Quetivel to take possession of the lands of Ailric the thegn, and with Roger came the Feudal System. Every man in England now had a lord over him, from whom he received his land, and to whom he owed service. If Wadel the cottager was Roger's man, Roger in his turn was the man of Fitzgilbert, one of the great barons, and Fitzgilbert himself was the man of the King. But the question arose, How did Peter the priest fit into this system? Was he vassal of Roger or of the King, or did he occupy an independent position? England was now flooded with foreign ecclesiastics. One by one, all the bishoprics passed into Norman hands. Normans became abbots of most of the large monasteries. In many parishes the new landholders appointed Norman priests. And all these foreigners regarded the Pope as the Church's commander-in-chief. In the ninth century a Book of Decretals had suddenly made its appearance, which claimed to contain letters from the earliest bishops of Rome. Its aim was to prove that in primitive times the Church of Rome ruled all other Churches, and that this authority had been given by Christ Himself. The book was an impudent forgery, but the age was not critical; in France and Italy these Decretals were accepted as genuine, and the Norman clergy had learnt to consider themselves as men of the Pope, bound to look to him for orders and to obey without question. This made a conflict between Church and State inevitable, but, while William and Lanfranc, his archbishop, lived, the quarrel was avoided, and Durford's chief interest was its new church.

Norman Churchbuilding

The Normans were mighty builders. Partly as a thank-offering, partly no doubt to enhance the dignity of the manor, many of the new lords rebuilt the parish churches. Roger soon pulled down the little Saxon church, and built one in the form of a cross, with a low square central tower, like a castle keep, from which the curfew pealed out over the village every evening. Inside, the general impression was one of enormous solidity. The round-topped arches rested, not on columns, but on rounded masses of masonry. The narrow, round-headed windows without shafts or mouldings were little more than slits in the massive wall. Nowhere was any sign of carving, except such rough ornamentation as could be hewn with an axe, for the use of the chisel was as yet unknown; but walls and pillars alike glowed with red and green and gold. The rush-strewn floor had little furniture – no seats, save a stone bench for the aged running round the wall, no pulpit, no lectern, no communion rails: but a stone screen divided the chancel from the nave; a tub-shaped font stood near the door without base or pediment, its flat lid carefully locked to keep the witches from the water; and God's Board at the east end, a large slab of freestone[1] with a sealed cavity containing the relics, without which no altar could be consecrated. Such was the church in which Durford worshipped for the next three centuries.

Anselm and Rufus

When the building was finished, there was no Archbishop

[1] Stone altars were a Norman innovation. In Celtic and Anglo-Saxon times they had been made of wood.

to consecrate it, for Lanfranc was dead, and William Rufus was keeping the see vacant, and using the income for his own vices. But one day (1093) the news came that the Red King had thought himself dying, and, with the terrors of hell before him, had appointed the holiest man in Europe as Archbishop of Canterbury. Anselm, Abbot of Bec in Normandy, was regarded by all as a saint – it was said that the water in which he washed had power to heal the sick – but by training and sympathy he was a foreigner, knowing nothing of the laws and customs of the English Church. Rufus was a foul-mouthed, foul-minded sinner, but in the struggle that arose, the King was in the right, and the Saint was in the wrong; for Anselm declared that he must refer all doubtful matters to the Pope, but Rufus replied that this was contrary to the customs of the realm. The end was that the Archbishop had to go into exile. Durford wept, as it watched him pass through the village on foot; at night men pointed to a comet in the sky as a sign of the wrath of God; but by fixing men's minds upon Rome as the central Court of Appeal, he was forging heavy fetters for the church he ruled. For the Red King was but a man, destined to perish miserably in a few years time; the English courts would soon recover their reputation for justice; but Rome remained for centuries the corruptest court in Christendom, the court where the most successful advocate was always "the little round pleader who never spake", the court where the verdict ever depended on the number of coins in the purse.

Anselm and Henry I

When Henry I came to the throne (1100), he invited Anselm to return; but this proved only the beginning of a new controversy; for Anselm declined to do homage for his fief, asserting that a bishop could not be a layman's vassal. The King replied that no foreigner could hold office in England, until he had sworn to be loyal to the throne. Once more the Archbishop had to go into exile; but, when at last (1107) a compromise was arranged, the advantage lay with the Pope, for it was agreed that, though bishops might do homage to the King for their lands, all symbols of their spiritual authority should be received from Rome. In other words, henceforth every English bishop would have to acknowledge the Pope as his over-lord.

Then came the appalling reign of Stephen (1135-54), when, as the old chronicler records, "they filled the land full of castles and filled the castles with devils. They took all those they deemed had goods, and tortured them with tortures unspeakable. They robbed and burned all the villages, so that thou mightest fare a day's journey, nor ever find a man dwelling in a village, nor land tilled. And men said openly that Christ slept and His saints."

The Cistercians

But in the midst of this awful anarchy there sprang up a strange revival of monastic life. "In the short time that Stephen bore the title of King, there arose in England many more dwellings of the servants of God than had risen in the whole century past." In 1098 Stephen Harding, a Dorsetshire man, had seceded from the Benedictine Abbey of Moleme in Burgundy, and founded a new community in the midst of the marshes of Citeaux. The Cistercians, as the monks of this Order were called, were the Puritans of the Middle Ages. Their whole life was a protest against the luxury that had again invaded all the older monasteries. Abbots were spending fabulous sums in beautifying their churches. The clergy ministered in splendid vestments. The altars were covered with costly ornaments, blazing with gold and jewels. But in a Cistercian church neither tower, nor bell, nor stained glass window was permitted; no cope, nor tunicle, nor dalmatic might be worn; on the altar was only a linen cloth without any embroidery; above it one iron candlestick and a crucifix of painted wood. Elsewhere monks lived comfortable lives, keeping huntsmen to provide them with venison, and falconers to procure their pheasants, and they defended this on the ground that Mary must not degenerate into Martha. But the Cistercians allowed themselves only one meal a day; and then they abstained not only from meat, but even from fish and eggs; their only food was coarse bread and a mess of vegetables. In 1128 a little band of these monks crossed the Channel, and founded Waverley Abbey in Surrey, and in the next twenty years they spread with extraordinary rapidity through many parts of England.

A Cistercian Monastery

To this revival let us attribute the rebuilding of Durford Abbey. Nigel de Quetivel, Roger's son, felt that he was growing old, and feared to meet his Maker. Then he remembered that he was using land that had been given to God, that a minister had stood on the banks of the Dur before the coming of the Danes, and he sent to Waverley to ask for monks, promising to build all they required, and to endow them with the lands that had belonged to the minster. A small company of gaunt, white-robed men arrived, very different from the sleek Benedictine monks of Canterbury. In a peaceful spot among the woods the abbey church arose, stern and fortress-like without, but, within, inexpressibly solemn, with its pale grey nave and vast round columns and absence of all adornment. Here the brethren met for worship eight times a day. South of the church was a square green lawn, and on the further side the Fratry, where the monks ate their meals in silence. East of the lawn was the Chapter-house, or council-chamber of the monastery, and the Guest-house, in which any visitor was made welcome for forty-eight hours. West of the lawn was the long bare Dormitory and the Infirmary, and the Almonry, where food and clothing were doled out to the poor. Round the inner side of all these buildings, linking them together, ran the cloisters in which most of the work of the house was done. Here each monk had his own seat; here, winter and summer alike, in spite of the draughts that came in through the unglazed openings, he sat and wrote and studied; here the novice-master trained the novices and the cantor taught his chanting; here the cellarer and the chamberlain made up their accounts. The whole settlement was surrounded by a ten-foot wall. Outside this a new village gradually sprang up – Monksland was the name people gave it – in which the servants and retainers of the monastery lived, and a new road was trodden through the forest by travellers, who turned aside to seek the monks' hospitality. Indeed so many travellers turned in that direction, that within a few years the monastery was almost bankrupt; and, to extricate it from its difficulties, Nigel endowed it with the tithes of Durford. John, the priest, ceased to be rector of the parish: he became merely the vicar or representative of the abbey; seven-eighths of his income was appropriated by the monks, and he was left to live, as best he could, on the lesser tithes, the funeral fees, and small casual offerings. And this was no isolated case. The Cistercians were doing the same thing throughout the whole of England.

Becket and Benefit of Clergy

Stephen the Feeble was succeeded (1154) by strong-minded Henry II, and then came another stage in the struggle between Church and State. In 1162 all Durford was scandalized by the news that, "in spite of the protest of the whole realm and the groaning of the Church of God," the King had constrained the monks of Canterbury to elect his chancellor as archbishop. Thomas Becket was a skilful diplomatist, a dashing and successful soldier, but his whole life had been entirely secular, and moreover he was only in deacon's orders. But he was not the man to do anything by halves. Now that he was a bishop he did with vehemence all that the ideal bishop of those days was expected to do. He rose before dawn. He was scourged daily. He caused his food to be boiled in fennel, to render it unpalatable. He wore a hair-shirt next his skin, and rejoiced when it became infested with vermin. Above all, he became an unbending champion of the papal idea of the rights of the Church. Now Henry was striving to reorganize justice after Stephen's anarchy, and the chief obstacle in his way was the existence of the ecclesiastical courts. These claimed to decide, not only Church questions including marriage and wills, but also all criminal cases in which a "cleric" was concerned, a term which included door-keepers and singing-men and all in minor orders. Punishments in Church courts were generally light. The bishops had prisons, but they seldom used them, as they naturally disliked the expense of maintaining prisoners. The usual penalties were penance or excommunication. This "benefit of clergy", as it was called, led to grave abuses. The judges reported that in nine years a hundred murderers had in this way escaped punishment, and Henry made the reasonable demand, that clerics, found guilty in the Church courts of offences against the criminal law, should be deprived of their orders, and handed over to the King's judges to be dealt with as laymen. But Becket declined to surrender a single privilege of the Church: and most men in Durford sympathized with him, for the King's judges were everywhere hated for the hideous ferocity of their sentences. Three councils were held, at each of which the dispute grew more bitter. Then news came (1164) that Becket had been driven from the King's presence as a traitor. It was whispered that he was hiding in the neighbouring village of Eastry. Then it was known that he had escaped from Sandwich to Flanders. For the next six years Canterbury was without an archbishop.

Murder of Becket

At last (1170) peace was patched up, and Becket landed once more at Sandwich. His ride to Canterbury was a triumphal procession. From Durford and every village on the road priests and parishioners met him in procession with their crosses. The people stripped off their garments and strewed them in the way. The air rang with the cry "Christ wins!" "The Bride of Christ conquers!" But the triumph was a short one. Becket had returned in no conciliatory mood. Before leaving France he had excommunicated the Archbishop of York for presuming to crown the Prince of Wales in his absence, a privilege which he declared belonged exclusively to the See of Canterbury. When the King heard of this new dispute, he lost all self-control. "What sluggard knaves I have in my court," he shouted again and again, "that they suffer me to be bearded thus by one low-born clerk!" Two days later the archbishop was foully slain. Four knights had heard the King's words and secretly crossed the Channel. In the afternoon they interviewed Becket, and demanded with threats that he should withdraw his excommunication. At vespers they burst into the cathedral with the cry, "Where is the traitor?" The monks ran right and left to the crypt and the side-chapels, but Becket stood his ground. Pausing on the steps leading up to the choir, just discernible in his white rochet amid the gathering gloom, he faced the intruders. They tried to drag him out of the cathedral, but he had been a soldier, and flung them off, sending one knight sprawling on the floor. Then they drew their swords and cut him down, and fled, leaving his body on the steps and his brains scattered over the pavement.

St. Thomas of Canterbury

The deed was not only a crime; it was a blunder. A thrill of horror ran through the whole land. Becket was at once regarded as a saint and martyr. On the night of his burial miracles began. A Canterbury woman was healed of paralysis by drinking water which contained a drop of his blood. In all parts of the land men and women began to see him in visions, clothed in white with the red streak across his cheek and brow, restoring to life pet lambs and even plucked ganders, helping to make the beer ferment, finding lost cheeses, assisting shipwrecked sailors to push their boat off the rocks. Three years later (1173) the popular verdict was confirmed by the Pope, and Becket was canonized at St. Thomas of Canterbury. The King realized that his cause was lost. Becket on earth had been a formidable opponent – Becket in heaven was irresistible. At last (1174), fasting and in pilgrim's weeds, Henry came to Canterbury, and knelt with bared back at the martyr's tomb, while the monks scourged him. The abuses of the ecclesiastical courts had to remain unchecked. Nothing would induce the clergy now to give up one jot of the claims for which St. Thomas died. For the next three centuries the worship of Becket was one of the most prominent features of English religion. In Durford Church the altar of St. Thomas against the side wall had always more lights before it than the altar of our Lord. Popular hymns prayed for salvation "through the blood of Thomas". Popular preachers, in amazing language, extolled the virtue of his blood. "Jesus," wrote one, "condemns all who drink His Blood unworthily: but gentler Thomas offers his blood not only to his friends but to his foes. Let all, therefore, drink of that blood who desire salvation." And to drink of that blood – or rather of water in which a drop of the blood was said to have been mixed – thousands flocked to Canterbury. Every day pilgrims used to pass through Durford – sick men bearing candles exactly their own height, penitents doing the pilgrimage barefoot and in hair shirts, foreigners from beyond the sea, even from distant Iceland. Back they would come a few days later, with little flasks of the precious Canterbury water sewn in their caps, rejoicing in the belief that their prayers would be answered.

Other Pilgrimage Centres

The Norman Conquest had not checked the English love of pilgrimage. Walsingham in Norfolk drew almost as many devotees as Canterbury, for there a drop of the

Virgin's milk was exposed in a crystal phial. St. Albans (1178) acquired a new attraction. A convenient dream revealed the fact that St. Alban's teacher, St. Amphibalus – the name was obviously coined from the Greek word for a cloak – was buried three miles from the city. The bones were dug up, and placed in a costly shrine, and a priest, who declared that these precious relics had raised him from the dead, was sent through England to advertise their merits. Durham had added to the banner of St. Cuthbert and the stolen body of St. Bede a drop of the Virgin's milk, the basin in which the Apostles' feet were washed, and a tooth of St. Gengulph, a powerful cure for epilepsy. St. Swithin's bones at Winchester, St. Joseph of Arimathea's thorn at Glastonbury still drew thousands annually. In the valley of the Alan was the tomb of St. David, two pilgrimages to which were reckoned as equal to one pilgrimage to Rome. At Reading was the hand of St. James; at Exeter the burning bush which Moses had seen in the desert. But Canterbury eclipsed them all in the splendour of its relics. Round the shrine of St. Thomas were twelve complete skeletons of canonized saints, three skulls, eleven arms, and four hundred thighs, thumbs, teeth, toes, and jawbones; here, too, was part of the Bethlehem manger and of the Virgin's bed, and of the Table of the Lord's Supper; here was Aaron's rod that budded, and, more marvellous still, the actual clay out of which God had moulded Adam. For saints and sinners, sick and strong, rich and poor, old and young, pilgrimage was regarded as the most effectual of all the means of grace.

The Interdict

For nearly forty years there was little to disturb the current of Church life in Durford, save for the departure (1189) of one or two of the more restless spirits with King Richard to the Crusade. But in March, 1208, an event occurred of a most astounding character. That contemptible little scoundrel King John now sat on the throne, and for some time there had been rumours of trouble between him and the Pope. The Archbishopric of Canterbury was vacant. The younger monks had chosen one man; the King and the elder monks had chosen another (1205). The Pope had quashed both elections, and compelled the monks, who had gone to Rome, to elect Stephen Langton (1206), but the King had refused (1207) to allow him to land in England. So matters stood on Passion Sunday, 1208, as Durford people quietly climbed the hill to church; but there was no Mass celebrated that morning. Instead, Osborn, the priest, read a paper announcing that the Pope had laid the kingdom under an interdict. The whole land was to be treated as abhorred of God and forsaken. Altars were to be stripped, church doors locked, no public services of any kind permitted. The dead were to be buried in silence in unconsecrated ground. For the first time for ten centuries the voice of praise and prayer was silent from one sea to the other, and this state of things continued for more than six years. It was a blind and fatuous proceeding. The work of the Church was utterly crippled; Christian people were deprived of all the means of grace; many a ploughman never recovered the habit of public worship; and the only man who cared nothing was the lustful and blasphemous little King; he never went to church, when the churches were open, and the interdict gave him an excuse for confiscating the goods of the clergy. It was even rumoured – and the story was believed by the monkish chroniclers – that he meant to retaliate by turning Mohammedan, and suppressing the Christian religion, and that he had sent an embassy to the Moors to arrange the matter. The Pope's next move, in 1212, was to pronounce that John was deposed from his throne, and to invite King Philip of France to carry out the sentence. Then John collapsed, like the craven that he was. In blind panic he made the most abject submission. He grovelled at the feet of the Papal Legate, and surrendered to the Pope his kingdom and his crown. "Let all men know," so ran his certificate, "that the King has subjected England and Ireland to the Holy Roman Church, and has given his territories to God and to the Lord Pope. He and his heirs are to hold them of the Lord Pope and his successors. Publicly and before everyone he has done fealty to the Holy Roman Church, and sworn homage on the Gospels." Innocent III had won what many generations of Popes had worked for. The Bishop of Rome was now Lord Paramount of England.[1] If John received his kingdom back, it was only as a papal vassal, and on condition that he paid a tribute of a thousand marks a year. The head of the feudal system in England was now the Pope, for the King had become the Pope's man. A Papal Legate now took up his residence in England. Vacant benefices were filled by him without any reference to the wishes of bishops or patrons. When Archbishop Langton ventured to protest he was excommunicated. For the rest of his evil life, until the feast of beer and peaches freed the land from his oppression, John remained in very fact the "most humble and most obedient servant" of his "holy lord and father". "Truly believing," he wrote to the Pope, "that the defence of us and the kingdom, which is yours, is committed to your holiness, we do resign that care and anxiety to your lordship; to your holiness we commit the authority that we have over all things belonging to us and our realm, and we will hold ratified and established, whatever you shall think fit to ordain". Nor must we imagine, as is sometimes asserted, that indignation at this surrender is a modern sentiment. "Woe to thee, John," wrote Matthew Paris (c. 1236), "thou of sad memory for all future ages! Thou

[1] The famous first clause in the Great Charter, which John signed two years later (1215), "that the Church of England be free," was sometimes quoted in later times in an anti-papal sense. But its original meaning undoubtedly was free from royal interference, free to obey the ecclesiastical authorities and the Roman court, without any control from the civil government of the country, the kind of freedom that Becket died for, and that the Pope above all things desired.

wast free, but thou hast made thyself a vassal of slavery, and hast involved thy most noble land with thee in the charter of slavery. And what of thee, O Pope! who oughtest to shine to the whole world as the defender of justice, the guardian of truth – dost thou defend such a man, that all things may be sunk in the gulf of Roman avarice? Thy doings and thine excuses for them are thine accusation before God."

Chapter 5

How men tried to reform the Church from without and from within

Papal Claims

THE Church's work was now hampered by many tangled problems. There was first the serious political problem caused by the claim of the Pope to control the secular government. Henry III, when he came to the throne, was only a child of nine, and Gualo, the Pope's Legate, seized supreme power. When peace was made with France, Gualo signed the treaty first as the Pope's representative, and Henry, the Pope's vassal, meekly signed below. "The Kingdom of England is known to belong specially to the Roman Church." "It forms part of the patrimony of St. Peter." "The English King is specially subject to the Roman See": these were axioms which the Pope asserted to be beyond dispute. Many letters from Pandulph, the next Legate, have survived, ordering provisions for the Tower of London, stopping the payment of money from the Exchequer "without our command and special licence", forbidding the fortification of Marlborough, issuing instructions for the release of prisoners, the custody of castles, the collection of taxes, and a hundred other purely secular matters. Even when the King came of age, Rome remained supreme, for Henry was a timid, superstitious man, who seldom dreamed of disobeying his overlord the Pope.

Papal Exactions

Then there was the ecclesiastical problem, which arose from the Pope's practice of giving many English livings to non-resident foreigners, and of crushing with taxation those clergy who were resident. At Durford, for example, John de Guilton, the unfortunate vicar, had always been a poor man, for the monks had appropriated his tithes, but now he was reduced to beggary by the exactions of Rome. The Popes, through their constant wars, were head over ears in debt, and they turned to the English clergy, whenever creditors became pressing. Sometimes they demanded a tenth of their income, sometimes a fifth, sometimes as much as a third, and the money had to be forthcoming under penalty of excommunication. Often an additional tenth was claimed on the plea of a crusade, and all the Pope's private quarrels were now termed "crusades"; till at last John de Guilton had to pawn the Church plate to the Jews, and even then he could not raise all that was required. When he died, Durford was given a vicar whom it never set eyes on. Martin de Mantua was a dissolute young Roman, the son of a minor secretary at the Papal Court, and his father secured for him the vacant living. He was only one among hundreds of Italians whom the Pope was appointing to English benefices; sometimes they were officials of his court for whom he wished to provide an income; sometimes they were relatives of prominent Romans, whom he wished to conciliate; often they were laymen; sometimes they were children; whoever they were, they never set foot in England, but their fees and dues were regularly collected and sent to them abroad. In 1248, when the royal revenue was 20,000 marks, no less than 60,000 marks was being sent out of the country yearly to these foreign pensioners; by 1253 the amount had risen to 70,000 marks.

Appeals to Rome

In the third place there was a serious moral problem. The system of appeals to Rome had paralysed the authority of the bishops. Many of the monasteries were respectable, but there were flagrant exceptions. Most of the clergy were living lives at least no worse than their parishioners, but black sheep were numerous. If any bishop, however, attempted to prosecute an offender, the latter at once appealed to Rome, and the bishop was powerless. For example, the register of Bishop Grandisson of Exeter declares, that in 1332 the Prior of Barnstaple was "living a life enormously dissolute, begetting a family and bringing it up notoriously at the expense of the Church"; but the Bishop failed to get him removed. In 1333 the Abbot of Tavistock was a drunkard, "leading a life detestable to God and man". It took five years to get rid of this man, and then his successor "consorted day and night with persons of suspected morals" and wasted the funds of the monastery on his huntsman and his hounds. In 1334 the Bishop tried to get rid of the Prior of St. James's, Exeter, who had been "ofttimes convicted of embezzlement and fornication", but he failed, though the church was in ruins and the services discontinued.

Monks as Landowners

In the fourth place an agrarian problem was rapidly coming to a crisis. One-third of the land in England now belonged to the monks. They were hard landlords, as corporations almost always are, slow to adopt new ideas and strict in exacting the last legal farthing. The lay landowners were gradually dropping many of the more vexatious of the petty feudal burdens, but every monastery retained them. The monks were hated by their tenants and disliked by other landowners. Already men had begun to ask why so much land should be wasted in keeping in comfort a comparatively small body of idlers, who were doing nothing for the country in return. Two hundred years before the Reformation the dissolution of the monasteries was a proposal constantly brought forward, whenever Catholic laymen spoke their minds freely.

The Coming of the Friars

The first to attempt reform were the Grey Friars. In 1224 there passed through Durford nine mysterious strangers.

They had landed at Dover the day before; at night they had been arrested as lunatics; but next morning they had been released as apparently harmless. They were barefooted beggars, friendless and penniless, wearing nothing but one grey garment, ragged and patched with sackcloth, as befitted followers of Francis, that young merchant of Assisi who, eighteen years before, had abandoned home and fortune in order to follow literally in the steps of Christ. The Son of God made Himself poor. The Son of God, to serve men better, became a homeless wanderer. Francis determined that he would do the same. "Sell all that thou hast, and give to the poor." "Take nothing for your journey, neither bread nor money" – these were commands that he obeyed to the last letter. He humbled himself and became one of the lowest of the low. The lepers, the beggars, the city outcasts were his chosen companions. He lived with them. He washed their sores. He shared their filthy straw and their mouldy crusts. The story of what he was doing fired others to follow his example. Soon the Franciscan Brotherhood, as it was called from its leader, spread beyond Italy to France and Germany and Spain. Its members all took "poverty as their bride"; they were wandering preachers, ever on the move, servants of the poorest of the poor, pledged to possess neither home nor books nor money, begging their food as they went along, content, when they failed, to sleep fasting beneath the shelter of a hedge. Nothing could be greater than the contrast between the friar and the monk. The monk, to save his soul, withdrew from the world's wickedness. The friar, to save other people, threw himself into the world's wickedest places. The monks were governed on the feudal system of carefully graded obedience. The friars were a free democracy, organized by the citizen of a small Republic. While the monk was chanting solemn litanies in his stately chapel, the friar was drinking muddy beer with Piers Ploughman in the inn, or telling pithy, pointed parables to the beggars at the convent gates.

And now nine members of this Brotherhood had arrived in England.

The Work of the Friars

At Canterbury they were allowed to sleep on a schoolroom floor, and here five of them remained, while four pressed on to London. As soon as they had learned the language, they began to preach up and down the country in the open air. One of them would visit Durford every two or three weeks, and at first he had to endure a good deal of rough horseplay. "Some threw mud at them; others would seize them by the hoods, and taking them on their backs, would carry them about." But soon ridicule changed to enthusiastic admiration. Their good temper, their homely spirit, their cheerful self-denial, won every heart. Everywhere they were welcome. Multitudes flocked to listen to their sermons. A wave of religious revival swept through the whole land. Recruits pressed eagerly into the Brotherhood. In thirty years 1,200 Englishmen became Grey Friars. At least one bishop laid aside his mitre and one abbot his staff to throw in his lot with these shoeless preachers. "Your Holiness may know," wrote Grosseteste, best of contemporary bishops, to the Pope, "that inestimable service hath been done in my diocese by the aforesaid Brethren. They enlighten our whole land with the bright light of preaching. Oh, that you could see how the people run to hear the Word of Life, to confess their sins, to be instructed in the rules for daily life, and how much profit the clergy and monks take from the imitation of them."

Their Deterioration

But this was too good to last. Their popularity ruined them. It was not easy to remain humble when all the world was flattering. It was impossible to remain poor, when Queens and merchants, peers and peasants showered gifts upon them. The roving life was full of temptations, and, when recruits were admitted by hundreds, scandals became frequent. "It is terrible," wrote Matthew of Paris, "that in less than twenty-four years the Friars have degenerated more than the older Orders have done in three or four centuries. They have built dwellings which rival the King's palaces in height. They daily enlarge their sumptuous houses, encircling them with lofty walls, impudently transgressing the rule of poverty and violating the fundamental laws of their religion." The Canterbury Franciscans had a pleasant house on an island in the Stour, and from this they still went out to all the villages round, but when Friar John visited Durford, as he did about once a week, it was not to invite the people to whole-hearted service of Christ; he came as a mendicant, begging from door to door for the enrichment of his Order (evading the rule which forbade him to touch money by wearing a pair of gloves); he came as a quack doctor, offering for sale pills and nostrums to cure all diseases; he came as a pedlar, hawking pins, purses, knives, and girdles; his only definitely religious work was to hear confessions, and to grant a cheap and easy absolution; for, so one contemporary song sarcastically declares –

> Had a man slain all his kin,
> Go shrive him at a Friar,
> And, for less than a pair of shoon
> He will assoil him clean and soon,
> And say the sin that he has done
> His soul shall never dere (harm).

Before long the Friar became a byword for all that was sleek and lazy and sensual and corrupt, an idle vagabond, undermining the influence of the parochial clergy. So far from saving the unhappy Church of England from her troubles, their coming had only added another terrible scandal.

Revolt of the Laity

The next attempt at reform came from the laity. A young knight, Robert de Thweng, formed a secret society of "men ready to die rather than tolerate the Romans". Threatening letters began to circulate, sealed with two swords. On Christmas Day, 1231, Durford was delighted with the news that, in the neighbouring village of Wingham, where the rector was one of the Pope's Italian absentees, masked men had seized the tithe barn, and distributed the corn to the poor. For a time the foreign collectors fled for refuge to the monasteries, but the movement came to nothing. Six years later (1237) Matthew of Paris wrote: "Degraded creatures, void of morals and full of cunning, the proctors and farmers of the Romans, scrape together all that is of value in the country, and send it into distant lands". In 1243 stories were told of another secret society, which was watching the seaports, and destroying all papal letters. Certainly in 1244 a very much frightened man galloped through Durford with white face and jingling saddle-bags. It was Master Martin, the Pope's agent, flying for his life to the sea, to escape the barons, who had sworn to slay him.

Legislative Action

But with the growth of Parliament, lynch law of this kind fell into disrepute, and the barons and burgesses and knights of the shires began to trust to their new powers to check the crying evils. By the Mortmain Act (1279) the monks were forbidden to acquire another acre of land. *Circumspecte Agatis* (1285) ordered Church Courts to confine themselves to spiritual matters. In 1301 the Lincoln Parliament sent its famous letter to the Pope: "It is our unanimous resolve that our Lord and King shall not submit in any matter to your judgement". The Statute of Carlisle (1307) forbade ecclesiastics to send money out of the country. The Statute of Provisors (1351) punished with imprisonment any one who accepted a benefice from the Pope. The Statute of Praemunire (1353) punished with outlawry anyone who appealed to the Roman Courts on non-spiritual matters. But a wily ecclesiastical lawyer was more than a match for any Act of Parliament, and, since the earthiest of earthy causes could be made to appear "spiritual", the immediate result of this legislation was small. One thing, however, was accomplished. In 1366 the tribute promised by King John to the Pope was finally repudiated.

The Black Death

Meanwhile Durford folk had other things to think of. On St. Margaret's Eve, 1348, the great rain began. For two months it hissed and splashed without a single break, till the corn and hay rotted in the fields, and the cattle died in their stalls. When at last it ceased, the whole land was soaked and sodden and steaming. The woods were full of monstrous toadstools, green and black and scarlet. And then the plague came. Will Green growled one night at a boil beneath his arm. Next day he was covered with purple spots. Before sunset he was dead. Alan the priest, who came to shrive him, died the next morning. From hut to hut the infection spread, till the dead outnumbered the living, and poor, black, swollen bodies lay about unburied, and no leader remained – the Lord of the Manor and his steward, the vicar, the wardens, the clerk, the bellman, all alike had perished. From every village round the same story came. Monks and clergy, lords and peasants had been swept away by thousands. When the plague passed, it was not easy to fill the vacant livings. Probably half the clergy in England had died at their posts. Long Gregory, Durford's new vicar, was a hurriedly ordained deacon, who could not read Latin.

The Revolt against Serfdom

The Black Death caused many changes in our village life, but none greater than the fact that Ranulf de Quetivel, the new lord, found that he had not enough villeins left to till his fields, and was forced to hire free labourers. Now free labourers also were scarce, and many lords were competing for them, so wages rose steadily, till Ranulf and his friends combined in Parliament to pass the Statute of Labourers (1351), making it a crime punishable by branding with a hot iron for any labourer to ask or receive more than threepence a day. Meanwhile the villeins, who held land on condition that they did certain tasks on the lord's estate, when they saw the increased prosperity of the labourers, began to kick against the old conditions and to demand fresh terms. The result was constant bad blood, strikes, and local riots. Every year the lords grew stiffer, the peasants more stubborn and rebellious. In this crisis the Church, like the nation, was divided. The monks and bishops, being large landowners, regarded the spirit of revolt with horror and amazement. But the friars and many of the parochial clergy were enthusiastically on the side of the peasants. The Franciscans had long been denouncing wealth, and now there had grown up among them a school of mystics, who taught quite frankly that private property is sin, and that Churchmen ought to hold all things in common.

> They preche men of Plato and proven it by Seneca,
> That all things under heaven ought to be in commune.

John Ball

Many of the parochial clergy were influenced by this teaching, and amongst others John Ball. We would fain know more about this man, the first Christian Socialist leader in England. For twenty years we catch glimpses of him in the Bishops' Registers, a mysterious, hunted figure, deprived of his church, excommunicated, constantly arrested and imprisoned, but always reappearing, "slinking back," so the Archbishop complained, "like a fox that evades the hunters, fearing not to preach in churches and churchyards, using dreadful language". We find him in Yorkshire, we find him in Essex, but most often in Kent, and Durford would have received more than one visit from him. We can picture his tall, black-robed figure, standing on the white steps at the base of the churchyard cross, surrounded by a great crowd from all the villages round, thundering forth that the Pope was anti-Christ, that every monastery ought to be dissolved, that all men are brethren descended from the same parents, that social distinctions are always sin, the invention of Satan, that all who support this state of sin must be plucked up like tares –

> When Adam dalf and Eve span,
> Who was then the gentle man?

Administering Extreme Unction.
From "The Art of Good Lyving and Good Dying," 1492.

And, when he was absent, his quaint epistles were passed from hand to hand: "John the Priest greeteth John Nameless and John the Miller and John the Carter, and biddeth them stand together in God's Name, and biddeth Piers Ploweman goe to his werke, and chastise well Hobbe the Robbere, and take with you John Trueman and all his fellows and no more, and look always to one head and no more.

> John the Miller hath ground small, small,
> The King's Son of Heaven shall pay for all.
> Let right help might, and skill go before will,
>   Then shall our Mill go aright.
> But if might go before right, and will before skill,
>   Then is our Mill mis-a-dight."

The Peasants' Rising

And now the day for which John Ball and his friends were working was at hand. The Poll-tax of 1381 fanned all the smouldering embers into a fierce flame. News came that North Kent had risen in revolt, that Rochester Castle had surrendered, that the "Army of the Commons of England" under Wat Tyler had entered Canterbury, and sacked the Archbishop's palace. Durford, like other Kentish villages, was waiting for the signal to rise. First the Manor House was sacked, and every court-roll carefully destroyed. Then all the able-bodied men, with Long Gregory at their head, marched to Canterbury to enlist beneath the red-cross banner. Two days later they set off for London to make all crooked things straight, and to see the King, and to teach him to be little brother to the men who live in cots. Then came news that London had been occupied without striking a blow, the Tower captured, and the Archbishop beheaded as a traitor. And then Durford heard nothing, till the men themselves returned, tricked, cowed, and beaten, to await the hanging, the quartering, the disembowelling, the doom of those who had failed.

John Wyclif

Meanwhile another movement was beginning to make

John Wyclif.

itself felt. Hob, the son of Daw the Ditcher, had been a clever lad. As choirboy in the Abbey he had picked up a smattering of Latin. Old Jocelin, the novice-master, had taught him a little more. And six years before the Peasant Rising he had begged his way to Oxford, and become one of that noisy host of lawless chamber-dekyns, who split hairs and cracked crowns in the name of the Seven Sciences. Now he suddenly reappeared in his native village, bare-headed, bare-footed, clad in a dark red gown, announcing that he had become one of the Poor Preachers, a new Order founded at Oxford by Dr. John Wyclif. One or two even in Durford had heard of the fame of Wyclif, the greatest living teacher of philosophy, the idol of the Oxford students, that prodigy of learning, whom no doctor had ever defeated in debate. For years he had been attacking the corruptions of the Church, and now he was sending out his followers to spread his views among the people. When the villagers gathered round the cross to hear John Wyclif's message, they soon discovered that it was of a very startling nature. The Poor Preacher had six points which he constantly repeated:

1. All clergy ought to be as poor as Christ himself. "Prestis schulde by no way have eny possescyons." "All herdis (shepherds) of Christ schulden lyve on the almes of the sheep they techen." Laymen must disendow the Church, and set it free from the wealth that is choking its spiritual life. In other words, the Rule of Poverty, which St. Francis drew up for his friars, Wyclif wished to impose on all bishops and clergy.

2. Monks with "their great bellies and their red fat cheeks" squander the nation's wealth, and do no service either to Church or State. The true Christian life is a life lived in the world. Therefore all monasteries ought to be dissolved.

3. Friars are the seducing spirits foretold in God's Word, who were to spread through the world, when Satan was unbound. They draw men hellwards by the threefold cord of bad example, bad advice, and easy absolution. They should be driven from the realm and their goods confiscated.

4. It is quite possible for the Church to exist without any Pope at all. If there must be one, it certainly need not be the Bishop of Rome. Let that bishop be chosen who is most like St. Peter in holiness, poverty, and humility. It is clear that the existing Popes with their love of lucre and their lust of power, their castles and their mercenaries and their gaols are anti-Christs, Vicars of Satan, the Abomination of Desolation sitting in the Temple of God.

5. Holy Writ is the only true standard of life and doctrine, the supreme and decisive authority by which all Church law and Church tradition must be tested.

6. The Doctrine of Transubstantiation[1] is absurd and

---

[1] Viz. that by the act of consecration the bread and wine are miraculously changed into the Body and Blood of Christ, so that no bread or wine remain, and nothing is present but the actual Body of Christ, though it is allowed to look and taste still like bread and wine, "since it is revolting to the nature of man to be fed with human flesh or with a draught of blood".

blasphemous. To worship the Host as though it were God is nothing short of idolatry.

But for all this it must not be supposed that Wyclif's position was the same as that of the later Reformers. To him the Virgin was still the sinless "Refuge of sinners", without whose help and intercession no man could reach heaven. He believed that God's people had to pass through purgatory, and that their sojourn there might be shortened by masses offered on earth. He recognized as legitimate helps to devotion pilgrimages, relics, and images, though he did not place any high value on them. He rejected the doctrine of transubstantiation as philosophically unsound, but, in spite of all that he wrote on the subject, it is hard to understand what he wished to substitute for it. His way of asserting the Real Presence of the Body of Christ in the elements is often, even in his latest books, extraordinarily like the old doctrine stated in a different way. Above all, he never seems to have grasped the central position which the doctrine of Justification by Faith ought to hold in any theology that is based on the New Testament.

The First English Bible

His bold criticism of existing institutions gave a useful stimulus to thought and free inquiry, but the part of his teaching which really bore fruit was his assertion that no doctrine or rite ought to be received as necessary to salvation "save it which is grounded in Holi Scripture"; for he taught this not as an abstract theory, but "he filled up the cup of his malice" (so Archbishop Arundel complained) "by the device of a translation of the Scriptures into his mother tongue". "He translated into English," wrote the scandalized Knighton, "that Gospel which Christ committed to the clergy that they might adminster it gently to laymen and infirm persons. By him it is becoming more open to laymen than it used to be to clerks with a fair amount of learning. Thus the gospel pearl is trodden by swine." The Psalter and a few fragments of the Bible had before this been turned into English, but these manuscripts had never obtained a large circulation, and were in use mainly in nunneries. Greek and Hebrew were unknown tongues, even to the bishops. The only Bible[1] within reach of the ordinary priest or layman was the Latin version which we call the Vulgate. Now Wyclif and a few of his friends set to work to translate this Latin Bible into English. Their task was not yet finished, but Hob Dawson brought with him the Revelation of St. John, the first book which the master himself had translated, and in the evening, when the rustics gathered beneath Bet Brewster's ale-steak, he read aloud awe-inspiring portions of it to them:

"Y herde a voys fro heven seiyng, My people go ze out, and be not parceners of the trespasses of it, and ze shulen not receyve of the plagis of it. For the synnes of it camen unto heven, and the Lord hadde mynde of the wickednesses of it. Zelde (i.e. recompense) ze to it as she zeldide to you, and double ze double thinges aftir hir workis. . . . Wo! wo! wo! the ilke greet citie Babilon and the ilke stronge citie: for in oon hour thi doom cometh" (Rev. 18: 4-10).

The Lollards

Before long a change was noticed in some of the villagers. Their lives became stricter, their talk cleaner, than that of their neighbours round. It was known that these were the

[1] Modern Romanist writers have laid great stress on a statement by Sir Thomas More a century and a half later that "Ye hole byble was long before his (Wyclif's) day by vertuous and wel lerned men translated into ye Englysh tong". "Myself have seen and can shewe you Bybles fayr and old, written in Englysch, which have been sene by the byshope, and left in leymen's handes to such as he knewe for good and catholike folk." But if there was such a Version, why has no single copy of it survived, and why, in all the long controversy on Bible reading at the Reformation was not constant reference made by both sides to it, the Romanists to show the fair mindedness of the Mediaeval Church, the Protestants to prove that their opponents had once approved of Bible reading? The only explanation seems to be that More must have mistaken one of the two Wyclifite versions for an official translation, perhaps because some broad-minded bishop had licensed certain scholars to retain copies.

men and women who were meeting Hob in the woods, "Lollards" (i.e. whiners or canters) Bet Brewster's customers called them. In every village in England their numbers were increasing, sober, earnest men and women, studying the Bible for the first time in their own language, and striving hard to mould their lives and religion by it.

Sometimes curious dissensions arose, as to whether a Christian might eat pork, or might work on Saturday; sometimes the district was startled by some wild outburst of zeal, as when the image of St. Katherine was chopped up to boil cabbages; but on the whole they were quiet folk, mixing little with their neighbours, enthralled and fascinated by the Bible and by the communion with God, which came to them, as they studied it together. Wyclif died in 1384, and no new leader arose to take his place, but the numbers of the Known Men, as they called themselves,[1] grew steadily till, in 1395, they were strong enough to present a petition to Parliament, and to nail to the doors of St. Paul's Cathedral and Westminster Abbey the Twelve Conclusions on which their petition was based, conclusions which show that in many points the disciples had advanced considerably farther than their master:

I. When the Church of England began to dote after her stepmother the Church of Rome, Faith, Hope, and Charity began to flee.

II. The priesthood which began in Rome is not the priesthood which Christ ordained.

III. The law of celibacy annexed to priesthood leadeth to horrible sin.

IV. The feigned miracle of the Sacrament of Bread induceth all but a few to idolatry.

V. Exorcisms and hallowings of wine and water, salt, oil, etc., are necromancy rather than theology.

---

[1] From Wyclif's rendering of 1 Corinthians 14: 38: "If eny man unknowith he shall be unknowun" (cf. R.V. margin). Only those who knew the Bible were known to God.

VI. All clergy, both high and low, should be dismissed from temporal office, and should occupy themselves with their cure, and naught else.

VII. Prayer should be for love's sake. He who takes money to pray for the dead is not far from simony.

VIII. Prayers and offerings to roods and images are near of kin to idolatry.

IX. Confession, with the feigned power of absolution, enhanceth priests' pride, and tendeth to sin.

X. Manslaughter by law or battle is contrary to the New Testament.

XI. Vows of chastity by frail women lead to grievous sin.

XII. The multitude of unnecessary crafts used in our Church nourisheth sin in waste, curiosity, and disguising.

De Heretico Comburendo

The clergy were now thoroughly alarmed, and Convocation clamoured for stern measures of repression. In 1401 the statute book was stained with the Act *De Heretico Comburendo*, which ordered every heretic who refused to recant to be "burned in a high place before the people to strike fear into the minds of others". Even before it had finally become law, William Sawtre, the first Lollard martyr, was given to the flames. John Badby, a tailor of Evesham, was the next victim. Then came news (1413) that a great Kentish landowner had been arrested for heresy. Sir John Oldcastle was a knight from the Welsh marches, who had married an heiress of the house of Cobham, and come to live at Cooling. He had sent a Lollard book to London for illumination, and there it had been seized by the bishop's officers. He was tried, and condemned to death, but managed to escape from the Tower, and summoned all his friends to meet him in St. Giles' Fields. "You might see the crowds," wrote one chronicler, "hastening along by footpaths, by cross-ways, from almost every corner of the kingdom." What they meant to do, no one can say, for the King closed the gates of London (1414), so that their leaders could not join them, and attacked them suddenly on the night they arrived, before any organization was possible. "Many of thaym were take, and drawe, and hanged and brent on gallows." Sir John escaped for the moment, but was captured later, and roasted to death (1417) over a slow fire.

Later Lollards

Henceforth the efforts to crush Lollardy grew still more drastic. Archdeacons were ordered (1416) to search each parish twice a year for heretics. The King commanded sheriffs and justices to help in the hunt. The whole movement was driven underground, but it did not cease. William Taylor, a priest of Oxford, was burnt in 1422; Robert Hoke, another priest, suffered in 1425. In 1428 the Archbishop called a Council in London to discuss the alarming growth of heresy, and a priest named William Whyte was burned at Norwich for teaching that all good men have priestly powers, that a good layman may consecrate the Eucharist, that priestly absolution and auricular confession are unnecessary, that in the Blessed Sacrament the bread still remains. In the next three years (1428-31), 120 Lollards were prosecuted in the Diocese of Norwich alone. In 1431 an Essex vicar was burnt at Smithfield, and the Government was alarmed by rumours of a Lollard rising at Abingdon. In 1440 a priest named Wych, one of the Lollard leaders, was burnt on Tower Hill, and pilgrimages from many counties came to the spot where he died, till they were stopped by Royal Proclamation. In 1449 Pecocke published his famous work against Lollardy, "The Repressor of overmych blamyng the Clergie". In 1455 the Bishop of Bath and Wells complained to the Duke of Somerset that his tenants at Langport neither "dred God nor lyve by Holy Chirche", but minister the sacraments among themselves and refuse to admit a priest. In 1457 the Bishop of Ely unearthed a Lollard congregation at Chesterton with secret meetings for worship and their own preachers. In 1462 Wyllys, an itinerant Lollard preacher, was burned at Henley, and at Wycombe thirty-eight heretics were condemned to carry faggots as a sign that they ought to be burned. In 1466 William Balowe was burned on Tower Hill. In 1473 William Goose followed him to the stake. In 1475 the Bishop's Register lamented that there were many heretics in the Diocese of Bath and Wells. In 1486 nine Lollards were put to penance at Coventry. In 1489 two laymen were tried before the Primate for holding that the Eucharist is material bread, and that every good man is a priest. In 1491 the Bishop of Lincoln wrote that he was "Fatigued and vexed by many heretics", for "the insane opinions of the Wycliffists have infected many of the people", and Richard Petefyne was found guilty by the Bishop of Winchester of teaching that "the blessed sacramente was but a pece of dowe bakyn and prentyd betwyxt irones". In 1494 Joan Boughton, a widow of eighty, the first English woman martyr, was burned at Smithfield. In 1496 we are told "this yere many Lollers stoode with fagottes at Powles Cross". In 1498 many of the bishops were busy with heresy trials. There were burnings in Bristol and Canterbury, Norwich and Salisbury, and much faggot-bearing elsewhere. Twelve heretics "shryned with faggots" stood at St. Paul's Cross in 1499. In 1500 we have records of twenty convictions. In 1506 a large Lollard congregation was discovered at Amersham. Of the three pastors, one was burned in the town itself, sixty of his flock being forced to bear the faggots, and his daughter being compelled to set them alight; one died in the bishop's prison; and the third was taken to Buckingham, and burned in the market-place there. Of the congregation many were branded on the right cheek; others were condemned to wear a painted faggot on the shoulder for seven years. Two years later (1508) in the same town two more men were burned and thirty-three branded. Thus for more than a century we catch glimpses of this secret movement. We know little of its strength, nothing of its organization. But it is clear that in scores of villages there were companies of Christians meeting stealthily for worship in barns and sawpits and quarries, visited by wandering preachers, who passed rapidly from place to place with a price upon their heads, maintaining their protest against superstition, reading their much-thumbed manuscripts of the Bible, till they were able to repeat their favourite books by heart, preparing the ground for the Reformation that was soon to come.

Chapter 6

How Durford's sixth Church[1] was built and used

The Fall of the Tower

In our fourth chapter we watched the building of Durford's Norman church. But in that church today no one but an expert can detect the Norman work that remains: every schoolboy recognizes that the architecture is Gothic, not Norman. What is the explanation? The change was a gradual one. It began with a great disaster in 1222. The bells of Wingham and the bells of Ash had made the people feel that the credit of the village demanded that they should buy a peal also. So a big bell, dedicated to the angel Gabriel, was ordered, and cast, and hung. But the tower, like many of the Norman towers,[2] was already far too heavy, and the extra weight brought it crashing down in ruins on the top of the chancel.

The Early English Chancel

No attempt was made to rebuild the tower for the present, but the gap in the roof was covered over, and the whole parish turned its attention to the task of restoring the chancel. A new style of architecture had now come into fashion. The old Norman churches, impressive though they had been in their vast solidity and rugged grandeur

---

[1] Previous churches were (1) The wattled *eglwys* of the ancient Britons destroyed under Diocletian (2) the second British church burnt by the Jutes (3) the first English church burnt by the Danes (4) the second English church pulled down by the Normans (5) the Norman church.

[2] Norman towers were constantly collapsing, e.g., that of Winchester fell in 1107, of Gloucester in 1164, of Worcester 1175, of Evesham 1213, of Dunstable 1221, of St. Radegund, Cambridge, 1270, of Ely 1321.

Grouped Lancet Lights.

and stern disdain of ornament, were ponderous, dark, and sombre. Light and air were blocked out by grim, impenetrable masonry. Each arch and wall seemed to press eye and mind earthward. But the aim of the Gothic school of builders was light and height and brightness, roofs soaring higher and higher, windows growing larger and larger, arches no longer round but pointed, clusters of slim and graceful shafts instead of massive pillars, churches that would preach with every stone, "Look up! Lift up your heart!" This school was still in its first stage, the one which is called "Early English". In the new chancel every line led the eye heavenward, especially the lofty roof and the slender lancet windows with the sunlight streaming through their grisaille glass, and the round medallions of St. Thomas' miracles gleaming like precious jewels. And, since this was a mystical age, the builders made the walls slant a little to the south, to suggest the drooping of the Saviour's Head at the end of the great Sacrifice; to remind all, who could read their meaning, of the loud cry, "It is finished!"

The West Tower

The village then began to prepare to build another tower; and since this was a slow and very costly business, which might have to be spread over several generations, they abandoned the idea of replacing it in its old central position, and started work in the churchyard beyond the western wall. In this way no service was interrupted, until the Tower was finished, when, by adding a span to the nave, they joined it to the Church.

The Decorated North Aisle

Then came a lull in church building, till the reign of Edward III, when the great revival of religious life, which swept across Northern Europe, found expression in Durford (1330) in a desire to add a new aisle to the church. The aisle was built in the churchyard, and roofed, and completed, without in any way disturbing the older building. When it was finished, two slits were cut in the side wall of the nave, and in each a delicate pillar was erected. Then the arch between them was constructed stone by stone, enough of the old wall being cut away to slip each stone into its place. Not till it was finished was the old masonry inside the arch cleared away, and the aisle revealed. Two more arches completed the work, and the aisle was ready for consecration. Gothic architecture had now evolved the style which is known as "Decorated". Builders and sculptors had attained a more perfect mastery of tools and materials. The windows were no longer narrow lancets, but broad openings in the walls with stone partitions

Decorated Window.

flowing up into tangled nets of tracery. Each pillar shows the zest and vigour of the village craftsmen. Here is the tendril of a vine streaming in the draught from the door; here a saucy little squirrel sits munching a nut; here a wife is belabouring her husband; there a miser is hiding his purse; caricatures very possibly of well-known people in the parish. But why was the last pillar left unfinished? Why has that angel only one wing? and why does that spray of ivy end in a solid square? The Black Death slew the sculptors, and stopped the work. When men began to build again, it was in a different style and a less exuberant spirit.

The Perpendicular South Aisle

After the Black Death came the long drain of the Hundred Years' War with France (ended 1453), and the Peasant Rising (1381), and Jack Cade's Rebellion (1450), and the desolating Wars of the Roses (1455-85). It was not till England grew quiet and prosperous again under Henry VII (1485-1509) that Durford folk were able to think of further building operations. But then they noticed that the north aisle had made their church lopsided. Moreover, additional altars were needed for the new devotions that were now becoming popular, especially that of the Five Wounds and that of the Holy Name. So they decided to set to work to build a south aisle. They used the beautiful style of architecture which the monks of Gloucester had invented, to which our modern textbooks give the name "Perpendicular". Stand in Durford Church today, and glance first left, then right, and you will see in a moment the difference in the style. The glass-stainer had now become a more important person than the sculptor, and the aim of the later builders was to substitute glass for stone, wherever this was possible. Only just enough wall was left to hold up the roof, and everything else was turned into window. In the windows themselves the beauty of the stonework was sacrificed to the beauty of

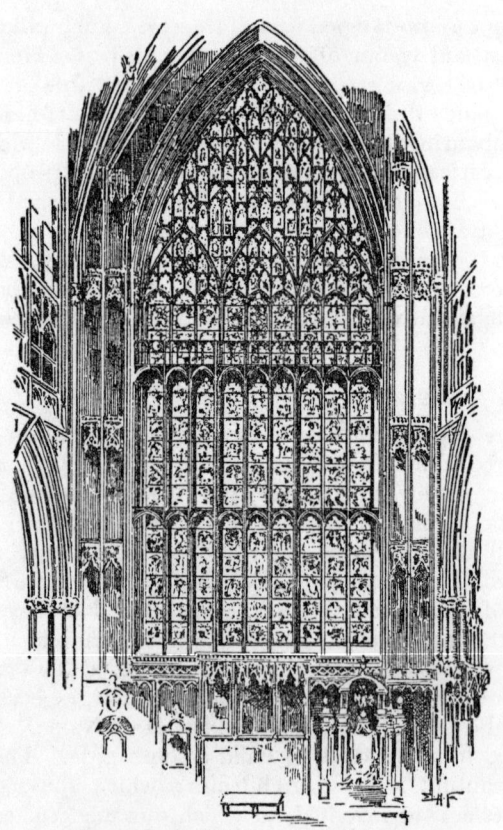

Perpendicular Window, York Minster.

the glass, and the graceful flowing contours and curves of the Decorated tracery stiffened into straight perpendicular lines dividing the windows into panels.

Clerestory and Spire

The church had now become so broad, that the old low Norman roof looked almost ridiculous, so the village boldly took it off, and added another story, full of per-

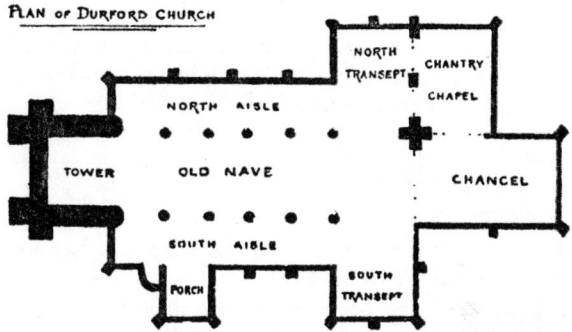

PLAN OF DURFORD CHURCH

pendicular windows, through which the sunlight poured into every nook and cranny of the building. But the raising of the roof made the Tower look squat and stunted, so a tall tapering spire was added, a great stone finger pointing heavenward, silently summoning the whole parish to seek those things that are above; and the fabric of the church at last had the form which remains to the present day.

Legacies

But how could one small village pay for all this building? The money was raised in a variety of ways. The fear of purgatory brought in a steady income. Almost every mediaeval will contains a bequest of some kind—an ox, a ring, a hive of honey, a gown, a spoon, a girdle—"that the preste be bownde to say *De profundis* for my sowle as oft as he saith masse"; "that they remember my sowle at every masse by name;" "that five masses be done for my sowle every Monday;" "that the preste, when he hath saide masse, shall stand afore my grave in his albe, and cast holy water upon my grave."

Pit Money

Then there was the Pit Money. For 6s. 8d. anyone could be buried inside the church, and for the sake of the

6s. 8d. it is to be feared that wardens often encouraged this odious practice. The whole church from end to end was packed with decomposing bodies, lying in shallow graves under the earthen floor, till nothing but the perpetual burning of incense made it possible to breathe in the building.

Miracle Plays

More important were the Miracle Plays. Let us visit Durford on the Feast of Corpus Christi. For weeks the village players have been rehearsing their parts, and now the whole parish is at church, as well as many visitors. Mass is over, and on a stage in front of the rood loft comes Sir Jonathas, a Jewish money-lender, and Sir Physicus, a quack doctor, infidelity and science conspiring to prove that "the belief of Christian men is false". A woman enters to borrow money, and is bribed with a bag of gold to go to Communion and steal the Consecrated Wafer. Jason, Malchus, and other Jews come in, and blaspheme the Sacrament. The woman returns trembling with the small white disc, and the Jews stab it with their knives. "Fools say that this is He that on Calvary was made red. Let us see if He hath any blood." To their horror it bleeds profusely, and the whole stage swims with gore. In a frenzy they try to destroy it. They scourge it. They hang it on a stake. They drive nails through it. They try to burn it in the fire. At last they cast it into a cauldron of boiling oil, but out of this there rises a life-size crucifix, and the Dying Saviour reproaches them in a long speech. Their shrieks bring in the neighbours, and Sir Miles, a Christian knight, kills all the Jews with his sword. "Then shall three or four devils snatch them up, and carry them into hell, and then shall they make a great smoke arise, and clash their pots and kettles." Then the Body of Christ again becomes a Wafer, and is carried reverently back to the Altar. Grossly irreverent much of the buffoonery would appear to a modern mind, especially the antics of the merry little devil Raggomuffine who was constantly banging actors and spectators unexpectedly on the head with his bladder; but plays like these appealed irresistibly to the rustic taste, and made the feeblest intellect grasp what Transubstantiation meant. Moreover they were a most successful means of raising funds. A successful play might bring in two or three pounds, which must be multiplied by twelve to give its value in modern money.

The Church Ale

A fourth regular source of income was the Church Ale. Just inside the churchyard stood the Church House, a long, low room with a large oak table, benches, and an open chimney. Here many kinds of festivity were held; the Bride Ales to provide a little fund to help young couples on their marriage; the Clerk Ales to raise the stipend of the parish clerk; the Bid Ales to help some poor parishioner out of a difficulty. But most popular of all were the five Church Ales on Candlemas, Midlent Sunday, Whitsunday, Allhallowmas, and St. Nicholas' Day. For these every farmer in the village gave his quota of malt, and the wardens brewed large quantities of sweet, light, hopless ale. The women baked cakes. Someone gave a bullock or a sheep. Piers Plowman had to pay to go into the feast; he had to give to the collection, before he was allowed to leave; and next day the churchwardens cheerfully entered in their accounts: "Receyved of our Ale at Whytsonday v. marcs xjd".

Hock-money, Plough-money, etc.

The Hocktide romping also brought in something. On Easter Monday the men stopped all the roads with ropes, and every woman who tried to pass had to pay a fine. Next day the women turned the tables, and took fines from the men. And all those were duly entered in the church accounts: "Receyved of Hock-money, of ye men's gathering vis. viiid., of ye women's gathering viis. iiid.".   Plough

Monday brought in rather more. This was the Monday after Epiphany, the day when ploughing began, and the young men after Mass yoked themselves to a plough, and made a house-to-house collection for the benefit of the church, ploughing up the ground in front of the doors of those who gave grudgingly. The wardens also made a few shillings by hiring out the players' garments to other parishes, by hiring out the church brewing-kettle for private use, by hiring out the bride-gear, a set of jewels which brides might wear at their weddings, by selling honey from the church's bees and wool from the church's sheep. When a specially expensive piece of work was in progress the parish agreed to a church collection for a certain number of Sundays. But even so the village could never have built the church it did, had not the stone and lime and timber been freely given by parishioners, and a great deal of the labour given freely too.

The Chantry Chapel

One addition to the church cost the people nothing. The dread of purgatory led rich men to leave land or money to pay a special private priest to chant daily masses for their souls. These chantries, as they were called, were very common at the end of the fifteenth century, and Sir Richard de Quetivel, who had gained great wealth in the wars, and was not quite easy in his conscience as to the way he had won it, built a beautiful chantry chapel on the north side of the chancel, divided from the rest of the church by a massive screen, emblazoned with the De Quetivel arms, in which he and his lady, carved in alabaster, would lie side by side after death, while every morning their own chantry priest would celebrate a special Mass to plead for their repose.

Churchyard

Let us now visit Durford Church as it stood in 1509, when Henry VIII became King. We pass through the thatched lich-gate, past the churchyard cross, past the ancient yew, which, ever since Anglo-Saxon days, has provided the people with so much that they needed—wood to burn for Ash Wednesday ashes, twigs to sprinkle the Holy Water, "palms" to wave on Palm Sunday, and bowstaves to defend their homes. We notice that all the graves lie on the south side of the church—the devil's territory on the north is reserved for the village sports—and we come to the south porch. Over the door stands the patron saint, St. Nicholas, Bishop of Myra. Just inside on the right hand is the holy water stoup. The porch itself is large and roomy, for here women are churched, and part of the marriage service held, and offenders put to penance. Above is a priest's chamber, filled with the parish armour.

Interior of the Church

The most striking feature of the church is its blaze of colour. Every square inch of wood and stone gleams with barbaric splendour. The wooden roof is turquoise blue, powdered with golden stars; the rafters are glaring scarlet; the pillars are a bright vermilion; the font a dark rich crimson; the pulpit and the doors a vivid green and yellow. The windows glow with coloured glass. In one the violet devils of the Doom are dancing in ruby flames, as they torture little grey-green souls, who fall from St. Michael's scales. In another the Tree of the Seven Sins grows from the mouth of hell, and in the branches sit purple Pride, blowing her own trumpet, and Envy gnawing a human bone, and Wrath with her bloodstained dagger. The great windows of the south aisle all tell the story of St. Nicholas. We see him with his burly figure and his broad red face recalling to life from the pickled pork-tub the limbs of the murdered children, boxing the ears of the heretic Arius, dropping gold into maidens' bedrooms, feeding the famine-stricken city.

The tints of the frescoes on the walls are every bit as crude and vivid as the lessons they suggest. Here is Hell

Cauldron, a red-hot pot bubbling on a blazing fire, in which a group of typical sinners—a lawyer with a writ, a friar with a purse, a peasant with a drinking-mug, a woman with an unclean toad—grimace in awful agony. Here is St. Nicholas once more, an infant three days old, solemnly refusing his mother's breast, because it is a Friday. Here on the north side, opposite the church door, are blowsy mermaids and pitch-black snakes coiling round St. Christopher's legs, as he struggles to bear the Christ-Child across the foaming river—a picture of marvellous virtue, for one glance at this preserves a man from sudden death that day. Here are three grim-faced skeletons warning three portly princes "As we are, so shall ye be". Against the pillars lean the banners of the guilds, richly embroidered with emblems. Here and there along the walls clusters of twinkling tapers reveal the presence of images of the saints, dressed in vestments of needlework.

The chancel is cut off from the nave by a carved oak screen, glowing with rich crimson and deep bronze-shaded gold. Above it is the rood-loft, with the great crucifix, that dim, pathetic figure with bowed head and wasted limbs, black with the dust of ages, the only relic that remains of the pre-Norman church. Inside the loft is the "pair of organs", from which the village blacksmith smites out the melody of the plainsong chants by blows of his mighty fist.

Through the rood-screen can be seen in the distance the High Altar, enshrined in saffron curtains, which are drawn right across the front at the moment of consecration. No ornaments of any kind stand on it, neither flowers, nor crucifix, nor candles,[1] but above, reverently shrouded in silk, yet clearly visible to all against its bright background of glass, hangs the silver Pyx, shaped like a dove, which contains the Sacred Wafer, which all but Lollards firmly

---

[1] During Mass itself one, or at most two, latten candlesticks might be placed on the altar, but they were removed with the other vessels as soon as the service was over. If the clerk held a lighted taper in his hand, no candlesticks were used at all.

believe to be the very Son of God. South of the altar stands the statue of St. Nicholas; north of it that of Our Lady of Pity with the dead Christ on her lap; at her side the Easter Sepulchre, a carved recess in the wall, where the Host[1] is laid on Maunday Thursday with all the pomp and ceremony of a mediaeval funeral, and left till Easter morning. At the foot of the sepulchre four stone soldiers lie wrapped in sleep; above four lovely angels wait with faces shrouded by their wings.

All round the church are other altars; that of St. Barbara who wards off thunderstorms, and St. Eloy, the horses' saint, that of St. Sebastian, the patron of archers, and St. George on his prancing horse, the new altars of the Five Wounds and of the Holy Name, and, still the most popular of all, that of St. Thomas of Canterbury. The pulpit stands where it is today, and the font with its gilded cover, but seats have only just begun to make their appearance; a few wooden benches have been admitted for aged and delicate women. The congregation stand or kneel on the rush-strewn floor.

The Ploughman at Church

How often did Piers Plowman worship in his parish church? Three times every Sunday:

> God's Service to hear,
> Both Mattins and Mass; and, after meat, in churches
> To hear their Evesong every man ought.

Mattins began at half-past six, Mass at nine, and Evensong at two, a short half-hour's service, the prelude to the village sports. Let us watch him as he comes to Mass. The Latin Mass was originally a congregational service, in which a Latin-speaking laity could take their full part; but this is no longer the case. Piers cannot understand a single word that is said, and the vicar, knowing that, does

---

[1] In earlier times a crucifix was laid there, but with the growth of the doctrine of Transubstantiation a Consecrated Wafer was substituted.

not trouble to sing loud enough to enable him even to hear. But Piers has been taught by heart some little English verses, and he kneels on the floor, and counts his beads, and repeats again and again the Paternoster and the Ave Maria:

> Father our, that art in Hevene,
> Hallowed be Thy Name with meek stevene (voice),
> Thy Kingdom be for to come
> In us sinful all or some;
> Thy Will be done in earth here
> As it is in Hevene clear;
> Our each day's bread, we Thee pray,
> That Thou give us this same day;
> And forgive us our trespass,
> As we do them that guilt us has;
> And lead us into no fondyng (temptation),
> But shield us all from evil thing.   Amen.
> Hail be Thou, Mary, full of grace;
> God is with Thee in every place.
> Blessed be Thou of all women,
> And the fruit of Thy womb, Jesus.   Amen.

Sometimes he lifts his eyes, and looks through the chancel screen, and watches the green-robed priest in his stiff, antique vestments, as he sways slowly backward and forward amid floating clouds of incense, kissing the altar, smiting his breast, doing awful and mysterious rites, which shall soon bring down the Son of God from heaven.   When the Sanctus bell announces that the consecration is completed, he bows his head to the floor and says:

> Welcome, Lord, in form of bread;
> For me thou sufferest hard deed.
> Jesu, for Thy Holy Name,
> Shield me to-day from sin and shame.

And then he prays for the departed:

> To all that in Purgatory pine,
> This Mass be mede and medecine.
> Forgive them all their trespass,
> Lose their bands, and let them pass
> From all pain and from all care
> Into the joy that lasts evermore.   Amen.

He never dreams of receiving the Communion more than

once a year – the Catechism has taught him, "Each man and woman that is of age ought to receive once in the year, that is to say at Paske[1] (i.e. Easter)" – but, when Mass is over, priest and acolyte come down to the chancel gate, and Piers goes forward with his fellow-worshippers, and kisses

A Mediaeval Confirmation.
From "The Art of Good Lyving and Good Dying," 1492.

[1] The Devonshire men, who rose (1549) in protest against the Reformation, included among their demands that none of the layfolk should be allowed to receive the Sacrament except at Easter. The practice of monthly Communion is occasionally mentioned in the Middle Ages as a miracle of saintliness.

the Pax, a small silver tablet with a figure of the Lamb, which the server holds, all that remains of the old custom of communicants kissing one another, and then he receives from the priest a fragment of the Holy Bread, a loaf provided by the householders in turn, to be blessed, not consecrated, and eaten by the people as a token of brotherly love.

Palm Sunday

But the service is not always so quiet and simple. Every festival has its own character and customs. On Palm Sunday, for example, first the branches of yew must be exorcised and blessed and censed and sprinkled. Then the priest comes down the church, arrayed in gorgeous vestments, bearing the Sacred Wafer in its silver shrine. Before it walks Jocelyn the clerk, with the jewelled cross, and half a dozen choir boys carrying horn lanterns. Above it is a beautiful belled canopy borne by stalwart yeomen. Piers and all the other villagers, bearing their "palm" branches, fall in two by two, and follow behind. Outside the porch they separate for a moment. The shrine goes round by the west end; the people, led by a blood-red cross, turn to the east. On the north side of the church they meet the Host once more, and kneel, and kiss the ground, while the choir sing, "Behold, Thy King cometh". And then they follow the churchyard cross, which they wreathe as for a victory. They pass back to the church porch, where the service is interrupted by one of those odd, incongruous incidents, so common in the Middle Ages. Someone on the roof throws down handfuls of unconsecrated wafers, for which the people scramble; – "al the boyes must be scuffling together by the eares, tyl al the parish falleth alaughing". Then with the staff of the crucifix the priest knocks at the door, and everyone enters the church, passing, as the children do when they play at Oranges and Lemons, underneath the silver shrine, which the two priests hold on high. When the Host itself is borne into the church, the large white linen curtain, which all through Lent has hung from the rood-loft, entirely concealing the chancel, drops to the ground. Then comes Mass, with every one watching for the Palm Sunday interludes, the singing of the long Gospel of the Passion from the rood-loft, a tenor taking the actual narrative, a bass the words of the Saviour, and the boys' treble the mockery of the Jews; and then the Prophetic Gospel, sung by three boys dressed as Hebrew prophets, a custom which explains the mysterious entry in the wardens' accounts: "For hiring of heres (i.e. wigs) and beards for the prophets, xijd.".

On Shrove Tuesday our friend Piers always went to Confession; on Rogation Days he helped to carry a banner through the fields; occasionally, when work on the farm was slack, he went to a week-day Mass, encouraged by the thought that every hour spent in this way was an hour added to life, for

> That day a Man devoutly heareth Mass,
> While he is present, he shall not grow old.

Such was the religion of Piers Plowman. His father and grandfather had done the same things before him; and in 1509 most men would have prophesied that his children and grandchildren would continue to do the same. Few realized that the Church was tottering on the brink of a religious revolution. Yet at least two-thirds of the rites and ritual of the Middle Ages depended on a firm, unfaltering faith in Transubstantiation. If that small round Wafer, so carefully reserved, were indeed Almighty God, then all these ceremonies and solemnities were natural and inevitable and delightful. But the time had come, when unhesitating belief in this doctrine was no longer possible. The long, persistent Lollard propaganda had raised a thousand doubts and difficulties, which could not be silenced. And moreover the reading of the Bible was producing a new type of religious experience, which could find in the old type of service no adequate or satisfying expression. A crisis was at hand.

Chapter 7

How the Church of England got rid of the Pope, the monks, and much superstition

Protestants before Luther

We have seen the Church go astray. We have seen reform thwarted. But at last there came a Reformation that did accomplish something. What was its origin? It is said by some that English Protestantism sprang from the wish of an adulterous king to get rid of an elderly wife; by others that it was born in Germany in the brain of Martin Luther; but a glance at dates disproves both these assertions. It was not till 1517 that Luther nailed his famous challenge to the church-door at Wittemberg. It was not till 1527 that Henry first mentioned to Wolsey his wish to abandon Catherine. But right at the beginning of Henry's reign the church authorities were fighting hard against a formidable revolt. In 1511, for example, the King's secretary wrote, "No wonder the price of faggots has gone up! a number of heretics furnish a holocaust every day, and the crop is still growing," an exaggeration, no doubt, but one based on a very grim reality. Watch how Archbishop Warham spent that summer. On 2nd May he condemned two men and an old woman to be burned; on the 5th nine men and four women were made to stand with faggots on their shoulders in the cathedral and their parish churches, and to wear painted faggots for the rest of their lives; on the 8th two more men were sent to the stake. Five heretics were put to penance on 15th May, four more on the 19th, two on 3rd June. A woman was sentenced to wear a faggot for life on 26th July, a man on 29th July, two women on 2nd August, a man on the 3rd, a woman on the 8th, three men on the 16th, three men and a woman on 3rd September. Meanwhile the Bishop of London was burning two men at Smithfield, and sentencing twelve men and women to wear the painted faggots. The same year a man was burned at Norwich, another imprisoned at Oxford; a priest was found guilty at Worcester; a large number of men and women were put to penance at Coventry. Next year (1512) Convocation was specially summoned "for the extirpation of heresy". Two years later (1514) the Bishop of London made a significant admission. His Chancellor was accused of murdering a tailor, who lay in the Bishop's prison for possessing "books prohibited by the law, as the Apocalypse in English, Epistles and Gospels in English, and Wyclif's damnable works", and the Bishop appealed to Wolsey to let him be tried by the Privy Council, "for assured am I, if my chancellor be tried by any twelve men in London, they be so maliciously set *in favorem hereticae pravitatis*,[1] that they will condemn any clerk, be he innocent as Abel". It would be wearisome to multiply examples. It is enough to state that there is ample evidence that early in the sixteenth century there was a bold and vigorous movement in many parts of England, not merely attacking questionable customs, like pilgrimage and relic-worship, but vehemently assailing the central doctrines of the mediaeval church, transubstantiation, priestly absolution, purgatory, and invocation of saints. The long Lollard propaganda was now bearing fruit.

Village Gospellers

The news from Germany in 1517 simply came as a stimulus and encouragement to men who had been working for years for the same end in England. "It is no question," wrote the Bishop of London (1523), "of some pernicious novelty. It is that new arms are being added to the great band of Wycliffite heretics." We have only space to illustrate this movement by one or two incidents. In 1521

[1] In favour of heretical depravity.

the Bishop of Lincoln made an onslaught on the Lollards of the Kennet Valley. Over two hundred were arrested, and the trials dragged on for months. It was proved that they taught that "in the sacrament of the altar was not the true Body of Christ, but a *token* of the Lord's Body". (Notice, we have here no trace of Luther's doctrine of consubstantiation);[1] that the "worshipping of images was mawmetry (i.e. Mahometry)"; that invocation of saints was useless, "What need to go to the feet, when we may go to the Head?" that "the Pope had no power to give pardon"; and it was said that "they had their instruction partly out of Wyclif's 'Wicket', partly out of the 'Shepherd's Kalendar' ". Six of the leading prisoners were burned; others were imprisoned for life in various monasteries; the rest had to stand with faggots in the market-places and churches of various towns.

University Gospellers

In Cambridge during the same year (1521) the University authorities confiscated and burned many heretical books, but every night the old-fashioned kitchen of the White Horse Inn was filled with eager students learning from Luther and St. Paul truths for which in later years many of them were to lay down their lives. The leading spirit was Thomas Bilney, a warm-hearted little man, who, after many miserable years of fastings, penances, and masses, had grasped St. Paul's doctrine of the Cross, while reading Erasmus' New Testament, and henceforth, till the day of his burning (1531), never rested in his efforts to open the eyes of others. Latimer, himself destined to be a martyr, has shown us Bilney at his work: "I was as obstinate a Papist as any in England, insomuch that when I should be made Bachelor of Divinity (1524), my whole oration went against Philip Melanchthon[2] and his opinions. Bilney

[1] The doctrine that the Body of Christ is present in the elements, "in, with, and under" the Bread and Wine; not however immediately after Consecration, but only at the moment of Reception.
[2] The friend and fellow-worker of Luther.

heard me at that time, and perceived that I was zealous without knowledge, and he came to me afterward in my study, and desired me to hear his confession. I did so, and to say the truth, by his confession I learnt more than before in many years. From that time forward I began to smell the word of God, and forsake the school doctors and such fooleries." Barnes, who was martyred in 1540, was another of Bilney's converts. He was Prior of the Augustinian Convent, and, as his church was outside the Bishop's jurisdiction, he was able to make it, till his arrest in 1525, a centre for "the new learning". Here Latimer began to preach with quaint and rugged eloquence sermons which convulsed the whole University with a storm of controversy, and many of the leaders of the Reformation in later years came from among the men who listened to his teaching.

Tracts and Testaments

Meanwhile in London a secret committee called the Christian Brotherhood, with subscribed funds duly audited, and paid agents travelling backward and forward through the country, was hard at work selling and distributing tracts. For the first time the printing-press was proving its power in England. Several of Wyclif's works were printed – hitherto they had only circulated in MSS – some of Luther's books were translated, new pamphlets were prepared, "Fifty Conclusions for Timid Consciences," "The Ploughman's Prayer," "The Sum of Scripture," even "A Children's ABC", and neither the Bishops nor the Government could discover whence they came. Then (1525) the King received a warning from Edward Lee, who became later Archbishop of York: "I am certainlie enformed that an Englishman hath translated the Newe Testament into English, and within fewe dayes entendethe to arrive with the same emprinted in Englond. I need not advertise your Grace what infection and daunger maye ensue hierbie. All our forfadres, governors of the Churche of Englond, hath with all diligence forbid and exchued publication of

Englishe bibles." That Englishman was William Tindale, an Oxford scholar, who had boldly declared three years before, when summoned before the Chancellor of Gloucester on a charge of heresy: "If God spare my life, ere many years I will cause the boy that driveth the plough shall know more of the Scriptures than thou". But he soon discovered that there was "no rowme to do this in all Englonde", and withdrew to the Continent. Here he translated the whole New Testament from the original Greek, and so well was the task accomplished, that every subsequent version[1] has simply been a revision of his work. Even in the Revised Version of 1881 more than eighty per cent of the words remain exactly as he wrote them. The first pages had actually been printed at Cologne, when the Church authorities discovered what was happening, and he had to fly by boat with the precious sheets to Worms. Here the printing was completed, and in 1526 copies began to be smuggled into England hidden in bags of flour and bales of Flanders cloth. Strenuous efforts were immediately made to suppress them. The clergy throughout the whole of England were ordered to hunt for copies. Blazing bonfires in St. Paul's Churchyard consumed all that were found. The bishops subscribed among themselves to buy up the books abroad, but by so doing they supplied Tindale with funds to bring out revised editions, so that "more Testaments were imprinted, and came in thick and threefold".

The Marriage Question

It was not till this point in the Reformation that "the King's Matter" began to have any influence. Henry had now (1527) been married eighteen years, but he had no son. His first-born had lived seven weeks, his second had lived an hour, this third was born dead. And now he believed that he had discovered the reason. He had married his brother's wife; and in the Book of Leviticus it

[1] The Roman Catholic version made at Rheims was the one exception until the mid twentieth century.

was written: "If a man shall take his brother's wife, it is an unclean thing: they shall be childless". True, before the marriage took place, a most elaborate dispensation had been obtained from the Pope, but Henry, who prided himself on his skill as an amateur theologian, knew that the best canonists held that the Pope could suspend the rules of the Church, but not the laws of God. So he and Catherine had been living eighteen years in sin! These misgivings seem in their way to have been perfectly genuine, but undoubtedly they were quickened by the fact that the King had lately been "bewitched" (the word is his own) by the black eyes and raven locks of Mistress Anne Boleyn. He applied to the Pope, not for a divorce, but for declaration that his marriage had never been valid, and under ordinary circumstances he would probably have got it; the Roman Church was very accommodating to kings in marriage matters; only a few years before a very similar decree of nullity had been granted to the King of France. But Clement VII was now a prisoner in the hands of the Emperor, and the Emperor was Catherine's nephew; so for two years the Pope shuffled and invented pretexts for delay, till Henry's very limited stock of patience was exhausted, and he swore that he would be master in his own realm, that he would recognize no appeals to any foreign judge. Wolsey, who had been in charge of the suit, was dismissed from all his offices. The Pope's name was erased from the service books. The payment of any fees to Rome was stringently forbidden. The clergy were terrorized into accepting Henry, "so far as the laws of Christ allow" as "Supreme Head of the English Church". In 1534 the position was accepted by Convocation that "the Bishop of Rome hath not by Scripture any greater authority in England than any other foreign bishop".

The Maid of Kent

Of course there was opposition, and round Durford it was fanned by the visions of Elizabeth Barton, "the Holy

Maid of Kent". She was a young farm servant with clairvoyant powers, who believed that the Virgin came to her in her trances, and gave her messages for the faithful. For several years she had been the pride of St. Sepulchre's Convent, Canterbury, and the monks and friars had used her revelations with extraordinary success to stir up enthusiasm for decaying superstitions. "Great stinking smokes" were made to issue from her chamber, during which it was given out that she was in conflict with the devil. "She spake many things for the confirmation of pilgrimages and trentals,"[1] and "she raised a fire", wrote one enthusiast, "like unto the operation of the Holy Spirit in the primitive Church". But now her revelations began to take a political turn. She declared that God had bidden her testify against "that infidel Prince of England", and warn him that, if he dared to touch the Pope's patrimony, if he married Anne, if he did not slay every heretic in the land, in seven months' time he would have ceased to reign, and she had seen the place in hell that was prepared for him. But the Tudors had a drastic way with those who opposed their will. The poor visionary and her chief supporters were arrested (1534) and hanged at Tyburn.

Visitation of the monasteries

Everywhere the monasteries were the chief centres of opposition. They were like hundreds of papal garrisons scattered through the country. But they were unpopular. Few regarded them now as homes of the higher religious life. No new abbeys had been founded for years. The ancient houses found it difficult to keep up their full numbers. Voices were asking why seven million acres of the nation's land should be wasted in keeping in drowsy idleness about seven thousand persons, who were giving back in return to the State no kind of useful service, and were suspected of being often scandalously corrupt. A century before (e.g. 1405 and 1410) Parliament had begun

[1] Trental, a series of thirty masses for the dead.

to call for dissolution. Wyclif had made this one of the points in his programme. Now Henry determined on a Commission of Inquiry. In the autumn of 1535, there arrived at Durford Abbey Dr. Layton, Archdeacon of Buckingham, one of the King's visitors. He inspected the accounts, made a careful list of all the Abbey's property, had a private interview with every monk, dismissed all who were under age, and departed, carrying his secret report with him. Many of this man's letters and minutes have been preserved, and the first question they suggest is, How could anyone in a few hours have discovered the personal and repulsive sins of which monks all over the country are accused by name? The explanation lies in the Chapter Meeting, which every monk in every monastery had to attend daily. Here every one was supposed to confess his sins in the presence of his brethren, and every one was expected to make known anything he had seen amiss in a brother's life. If Layton could only find one monk willing to talk about things unearthed in the daily Chapter, he would have no difficulty in compiling his terrible *Comperta*. And in most monasteries some one could be found who loathed the life, and hated his brethren, and longed for release. But are the reports credible, or must they be regarded as foul and shameful slanders? Let us grant that an enemy makes a bad witness, that the visitation was hurriedly conducted, that the visitors themselves were often men of infamous character. Still there remains plenty of evidence from sources above suspicion, such as the Visitation Returns compiled by the bishops in the course of their ordinary diocesan work, which proves that some, at any rate, of the monasteries were quite as black as they were painted. The Abbey of St. Alban's, for example, was one of the most important in the kingdom, yet when the Archbishop of Canterbury visited it in 1489, he reported that many of the brethren "neglect the service of God altogether; they live with harlots publicly within the precincts of the monastery; they have sacrilegiously ex-

Caricature of a Monk.[1]

tracted the precious stones from the shrine of St. Alban"; moreover they had infected with their own impurities two neighbouring nunneries. In 1514 the Bishop of Norwich visited Walsingham, the famous abbey to which pilgrims flocked from all parts of the world; he found the House ruled by the wife of one of the servants, who wore gold rings, and rode the prior's pony. The prior himself was living in adultery, his whole life utterly dissolute, dressing his fool up in a surplice and making him walk in procession. The canons were dissipated and quarrelsome, scaling the walls and spending the nights in taverns in the town. The whole place was a hotbed of corruption. At Norwich Priory, a Benedictine house of the first rank, which had absorbed the tithes of forty-three livings, the Bishop found (1514) that dances were given in the guest-house, that women were allowed in and out of the monastery as they would, that the sub-prior was a notorious profligate, and

[1] From MS. in British Museum (Sloane MSS. 2435, fol. 44). This is typical of the caricatures that abound in fifteenth century manuscripts.

that more than one of the monks was the father of illegitimate children. In the same year the Bishop visited the smaller Abbey of Wymondham. He found the buildings in bad repair, Mass and Matins neglected, several of the inmates habitual drunkards, wanton women in the monastery, and free fights in the cloister. When the Bishop of Lincoln visited (1515) the great Benedictine Abbey of Peterborough, he discovered the monks haunting taverns, dances held in the dormitory, and jewels stolen from the shrine of St. Oswald, and given to loose women. He lamented (1525) that the Cistercian Abbey of Thame was a scandal to the whole country-side. No repairs were done; the debts were immense; yet the brethren feasted riotously in the ale-houses, and the abbot confessed to being guilty of the foulest forms of vice. At Dorchester he found (1530) that the gates of the cloister were never closed, that men and women were admitted at all hours of the night, that the services were neglected, and that half the canons were either profligates or drunkards. From the bishops' own registers it is only too easy to prove that many of the monasteries were notoriously and scandalously vile.

Dissolution of the Monasteries

In March, 1536, Parliament passed a Bill suppressing all monasteries with an income of less than £200 a year (i.e. about £2,000 in our money); and that summer 370 were closed. Two years later the 200 Friaries were dissolved. But still at Durford the daily routine went on undisturbed. Cromwell, the King's terrible minister, seemed to have forgotten. But Cromwell never forgot. In the winter of 1538 the first blow fell. A letter arrived from the King deposing the aged abbot for "negligent administration", and appointing in his place the most unpopular monk in the abbey, the man who was suspected of having given information to Layton. Then a few weeks later a Royal Commissioner arrived, and the monks were summoned into the Chapter-house to meet him. With stern face he told them that it had been reported to the King that treasonable words had been spoken in their refectory during the Pilgrimage of Grace, the rebellion that had flared up in Yorkshire in defence of the smaller monasteries. He bade them choose between two alternatives. Let them show their penitence by surrendering their abbey into the King's hands, and every man should receive pardon and a pension. If not, the House would be seized all the same, but, instead of a pension, there would be a Bill of Attainder. The change of abbot had left them leaderless, and there was no resistance. With trembling hands they signed the deed, which was being sent round to all surviving monasteries, declaring "by our unanimous consent and free will we have given to our excellent lord, King Henry, all our monastery, as well as all our manors, meadows, markets, woods, and tenements"; and then they dispersed, some to seek work in the parish churches, some to find their way to other monasteries in Scotland or abroad, the rest to slip back into secular life. Immediately the work of destruction began. The plate was sent to the King's treasury. The bells were broken up to be recast as cannon. The lead was stripped from the roof and gutters, and with the help of the carved woodwork melted into pigs for removal. Windows, doors, timber, tiles were sold in lots by auction. The massive walls were left as a quarry, from which stones might be picked by payment of a few shillings. A little later the lands were sold to Martin Peke, a London merchant, who had made a fortune by importing spices. By the end of March, 1540, not a single monastery or nunnery remained in England.

Destruction of Shrines

The fall of the monasteries meant a great change in the popular religion. Gone now were the shrines that had drawn pilgrims from every part of Europe. No longer could suppliants bring their petitions to the tomb of St. Thomas of Canterbury, or St. Swithin at Winchester, or

St. Hugh at Lincoln, or St. Cuthbert at Durham. No more could men gaze on the Saviour's blood at Hailes and Ashridge and Westminster. No more could they bow before the Virgin's milk at Westminster and St. Paul's, at Walsingham and Shrewsbury, at Coventry and Dale and Durham. Gone were all the wonder-working images of the Lord's Mother, our Lady of Willesden, our Lady of Ipswich, our Lady of Penrice, the gigantic figure of our Lady of Worcester, and the little black Virgin of Muswell which had fallen from heaven. Gone were all the miraculous crucifixes, the Black Cross of Waltham which once had bled, the Cross at the north door of St. Paul's, which once was heard to speak, the Rood of Bermondsey which provided husbands, the Rood of Grace in Boxley Abbey which used to frown and smile. Alas! when the workmen pulled down the church, the wires and pipes were all exposed by which this latter "miracle" was worked! Gone were the statues which healed the sick. No longer would glands be cured by St. Curig, gout by St. Wolfgang, headache by St. Ottilia, toothache by St. Apollonia, sore eyes by St. Clare, sore throat by St. Awdrey. No more would quinsy be cured by water poured through St. Blase's bones, or ague by images of John Schorn, the priest who caught the Devil in his boot. No more would St. Leonard heal the ducks, or St. Anthony the swine. No more would St. Kynanoe's collar show who spoke the truth, or a woman's chastity be proved by her power to lift St. Rumbold's image, or pecks of oats be left before that bearded virgin, St. Uncumber, in hopes that she would hasten the death of some unwelcome husband. Every image "abused with pilgrimages or offerings" was to be destroyed: so ran the King's decree (1538); and it was done, apparently without resistance, except in the backward North.

The Six Articles

Now it is absurd to suggest that even a Tudor, by his own determination, could have effected such a change in the religion of his subjects. This revolution would have been impossible, but for the Lollard propaganda. But, if the Gospellers of Durford hoped that Henry was coming round to their point of view, they were much mistaken. The King had declared (1521) in the book that had won him the title Defender of the Faith, that Luther was "the most venomous serpent who had ever crept into the Church", and he remained of the same opinion still. He was violently opposed to any change in mediaeval doctrine or mediaeval ritual. As King, he objected to a foreign bishop ruling the English Church. As King, he was willing to suppress any obvious abuses, especially when their suppression was profitable to his own privy purse. But Church services and Church dogmas, these must remain unaltered. In September, 1539, Durford people had a very lengthy sermon. The vicar was ordered to read from the pulpit the Act of the Six Articles – the Whip with Six Strings men soon learned to call it – declaring that (1) if anyone taught or held that after consecration there remaineth any substance of the bread or wine he should suffer death by burning; that (2) if anyone held that the Communion ought to be ministered in wine as well as bread, (3) that a priest might marry, (4) that a monk or nun might marry, (5) that private masses for the dead were not expedient, or (6) that auricular confession was not necessary, he should forfeit all his goods and be imprisoned at the King's pleasure, and, if convicted a second time, be hanged as a felon. The Pope was banished, and the monasteries destroyed, but Protestantism was still a crime punishable by death. In the first fortnight after the passing of this Act five hundred persons were arrested for heresy in London alone.

CHAPTER 8

How the Reformation was at last victorious

Archbishop Cranmer

WHILE Henry lived, no more reforms of a sweeping character were possible, but Cranmer, the Archbishop, was known to be in favour of further changes. It is time that we made closer acquaintance with the man whose quiet influence guided the course of the English Reformation. In 1529, at the time of the great debate about Henry's marriage with Catherine, a gentle, studious College don was lecturing in Jesus College, Cambridge. He had not escaped the influence of the movement which Bilney had started,[1] and for many years had been a careful student of the Bible, and for four years had been praying in private for the abolition of the Pope's power in England. A chance remark in a relative's house, overheard by the King's Secretary, caused him to be summoned into Henry's presence. He had wondered why the King did not submit the problem of his marriage to the Universities of Europe, which were the supreme tribunals for the decision of scientific questions. If this great body of expert opinion decided that he was a bachelor, there would be no need to appeal to Rome to undo a marriage which did not exist. "By the mother of God," exclaimed Henry, "that man hath the right sow by the ear"; and his imperious will, which would not take a nay, dragged the shy, retiring scholar from his peaceful college, and plunged him into a whirlpool of foreign diplomatic missions. Four wishes later (1533), greatly against Cranmer's own wishes, the King insisted on making him Archbishop of Canterbury. "I protest there

[1] See page 94.

was never a man came more unwillingly to a bishopric than I." His mind remained to the end of the academic type, which weighs and deliberates and hesitates, till it has grasped every side of a question: his beautiful modesty made him over-ready to distrust his own judgement, over-ready to attribute the highest motives to other people. He was ill-fitted to be a statesman in those tempestuous times; the overwhelmingly masterful personality of the King dominated him; and often we regret that he did not take a more heroic line, especially in rebuking and refusing to officiate at some of Henry's marriages. But yet it is amazing how in his own department of the Church his quiet perseverance always gained its end. As his mind developed, so he gradually carried the Church with him,[1] and the man who could do this in the teeth of the Gardiners, Thirlebys, and Wriothesleys of that day was certainly no backboneless weakling.

The Great Bible

He now obtained permission to try another cautious experiment. This was the introduction of a little English into the Latin services. As early as 1538, Simon Winch, Vicar of Durford, had received an injunction: "Ye shall provide on this side of Easter one book of the whole Bible of the largest volume in English, and set it up within the Church, where your parishioners may most conveniently read it". But Easter came, and the following Easter, and still the Bible was not ready. Cranmer had not found it an easy matter to provide an English Bible. Tindale had been seized and strangled (1536), before he had finished the Old Testament. Coverdale (1535) had made a beautiful translation from the Latin and the German, but this was not based on the original texts. John Rogers (1537) had edited Matthew's Bible, skilfully combining all that was best in Coverdale and Tindale, but he had spoilt it by highly

[1] His only serious checks were the Six Articles (1539) and the King's Book (1543).

controversial annotations. Then Cranmer gave Matthew's Bible to Coverdale to revise once more, and at last he had a text that satisfied him. But the difficulty of getting it printed had yet to be overcome. All the best printing was still done abroad, but the Inquisition seized the copies, when they were completed, and destroyed them. It was not till 1540 that there arrived in Durford an enormous volume, for which the wardens had to pay 12s.; this they fixed to one of the pillars by an iron chain, and left it there on a wooden desk for any to read who would. "It was wonderful to see with what joy this book was received, not only among the learneder sort, and those that were noted for lovers of the Reformation, but generally all England over among vulgar and common people. Even little boys flocked among the rest to hear portions read."

English in the Services

Three years later (1543) an order came that a chapter from this English Bible was to be read aloud by the Vicar in the middle of the Latin service. Next year the harvest failed, and an attempt was made to revive the old processional litanies through the fields; but it was found that the people had forgotten the Latin responses, so Cranmer was allowed to draw up an English litany. This was a task in which he appeared at his very best. His deep piety, his wide learning, and exquisite ear for language made him without a rival as a prayer-writer. He took the old Sarum Litany, enriched it with petitions from many sources, Latin, Greek, and German, and produced the service as we know it at the present day, save that it contained petitions to the saints to pray for us, and a clause asking for deliverance from "detestable enormites" of the Bishop of Rome. But it might not be used inside the churches. It was written to be sung as an open-air processional.

Edward VI

In 1547 Henry VIII died, commending his soul to

St. Mary, and leaving money for masses "to be sayd perpetuelly, while the woorld shall endure". Most of the Council, who misgoverned the country in the name of his little son Edward VI, cared little for religion, but they saw that the future of the Church lay with the reforming party, and they determined to give a free hand to Cranmer. He was a man whose views had developed slowly. "Little by little," he said, "I put away my former ignorance. As God of His mercy gave me light, so through grace I opened mine eyes to receive it." And now he had reached a theological position not unlike that of Luther. At Durford, Simon Winch had been vicar for many years, a cheerful, easygoing man, no theologian, no active propagandist of any faith, but a genial church official, conducting services, administering sacraments, hearing confessions, shriving the dying, anxious to live at peace with all men and to avoid controversy. His parishioners were divided into three classes. Some, and among them the De Quetivels, clung fiercely to the old ceremonies; others – and of these Martin Peke, the London merchant, was the leader – chafed at the slow progress of reform, and called for extreme measures. The mass of the villagers were, however, men much like their vicar, regarding heresy as disreputable, but sufficiently touched by the Lollard teaching to be rather sceptical as to the use of many of the ancient customs, willing on the whole to let bishops and Government do their thinking for them, and to accept their decisions with grumbling but without resistance.

The Purging of the Churches

But now changes began to come with bewildering rapidity. Winch was summoned to Wingham to meet the King's visitors, and he returned with a Book of Homilies and a big list of Injunctions. He was a man who was always willing to obey those in authority, but this time they had set him a task both difficult and distasteful. Even the reading of one of the homilies every week at Mass proved by no means an easy matter. Here, as elsewhere, the village lads, knowing that they had De Quetival behind them, made such a "shovelling of feet, such huzzing and buzzing, that nothing could be heard". But some of the other Injunctions were far more disagreeable. The crucifix in the rood-loft was to be sawn down and destroyed. The quaint old frescoes on the walls were to be blotted out with white lime. The stained glass windows gleaming with the legends of a score of saints were to be demolished. In every churchwarden's accounts in England appeared such items as these:

For whytyng the churche	£ 6 13 2
To simon synckler for his cost in rydynge to London when we sold the great crosse	3 0
To harry the glassyer for all his werke	4 5 1
Recs. for the great crosse sold at London	9 10 0

Even now we can hardly think of such havoc without a pang of regret. But Cranmer was no Vandal. He knew that nothing less than this would kill the old superstitions. Belief in purgatory would never die so long as the walls of every church displayed its torments and its terrors. The worship of the saints would linger on, if ten thousand windows were allowed to proclaim the legends of their miracles and mercies. If the choice lay between pure religion and the preservation of certain interesting archaeological curiosities, there could be no doubt which it was right to sacrifice, even though it meant a shock to the feelings of old-fashioned folk in the villages. And this was only the beginning of the end. In January (1548) came an order from Cranmer that certain ceremonies were to be discontinued – the Candlemas candles, the Palm Sunday palms, the Ash Wednesday ashes. A week later came another order forbidding Creeping to the Cross and the use of Holy Water. In February came the first order for the removal of all images. At Easter the De Quetivel Chantry was abolished, and the chantry priest dismissed with a pension; and with the chantry went a multitude of small endowments. Some parishioners had left money for obits, i.e. masses for the soul on the anniversary of their death; others had left money for lights and candles. But all these funds the Government now appropriated to its own uses, to the indignation of Cranmer and all true reformers. "If the drones must be driven out of the hive," wrote Bucer, "why should wasps and hornets be let in to gorge themselves on its stores?"

English in Church

Meanwhile, the amount of English in the services was steadily being increased. One of the Injunctions (1547) had ordered the Litany to be used in church, kneeling, before High Mass. Another had ordered the Epistle and Gospel to be read in English. Then came word that the laity were to receive the wine as well as the bread – an order which necessitated the melting down of the slender mediaeval chalice and the making of a large Communion cup – and with the order came a small pamphlet containing prayers that were to be used. The Latin Mass was to be retained "without the varying of any rite or ceremony" up to the point at which the priest himself received the elements, but then he was instructed to turn to the people with the English exhortation, "Dearly beloved in the Lord," which remains in our present Prayer Book, and to read, almost in their present form, the Invitation, the Confession, the Absolution, the Comfortable Words, the Prayer of Humble Access, the first half of the Words of Administration, and the Blessing.

The First Prayer Book

All these changes paved the way for a complete revision of the Church services. At Easter, 1549, Simon Winch received a copy of the new Prayer Book. How eagerly he would scan its contents! The first thing evident was that it was all in English. "Al thinges," said the Preface, "shalbe read and song in the Englyshe tongue to thende yt the congregacion maie be therby edified." The next point obvious was that many familiar things had been omitted, some to gain greater simplicity – "our excessive multitude of ceremonies was so great, and many of them so darke, that they did more confound and darken, than declare and sette forth Christes benefites," – others because they were "so farre abused, partly by the supersticious blyndenes of the rude and unlearned, partly by the unsaciable avarice of suche as soughte more theyr owne lucre than the glorye of God, that the abuses could not well be taken awaye, the thyng remayning still". But for all this a closer inspection showed that the book was intensely conservative. The old vestments, the unleavened wafers, prayers for the dead, were retained. The daily morning and evening services were not new compositions; they were portions of the old Latin offices of Mattins and Lauds, Vespers and Compline, clothed in fresh beauty by Cranmer's silvery English.[1] The Communion service contained many of the Missal prayers, together with those issued in the previous year.

The Second Prayer Book

The new book was not popular. Old-fashioned people disliked changes of any kind, and the Government complained that "a great number of people do wilfully refuse to come to their parish churches". The Gospellers, on the other hand, were disappointed that the changes were not more drastic. They agreed with Bishop Hooper that the book was "in some respects manifestly impious". As a compromise it satisfied nobody, and soon preparations began to bring out a revised edition. This reached Durford in October, 1552, and was used for the first time on All Saints' Day. It was far more Protestant than its predecessor. The word Mass and the word Altar were removed from its pages; the altars themselves had been removed two years earlier (1550) and

---

[1] They were almost the same as the middle portions of our present Morning and Evening Prayer, beginning with the first Lord's Prayer and ending with the third collect.

"one decent table" provided instead; the minister was directed to wear "neither alb, vestment, nor cope, but a surplice only"; instead of wafers, "it shall suffice" if the bread is "such as is usual to be eaten at table"; all prayers for the dead were deliberately omitted; the exorcising of the demon and the anointing with oil in baptism were discontinued. In general arrangement the book had now assumed its present form, though it was to undergo three revisions later.

The Reaction

This had only been used for eight months, when the boy-king died (July, 1553), and his half-sister, the sour and bigoted Mary, became Queen. She was the daughter of Catherine of Aragon, whom Henry had deserted, and her Spanish blood and her mother's wrongs caused her to hate the Reformation with fierce relentless hatred. The reformers had made mistakes and enemies. Their cause had been compromised by the shameless greed of the lay politicians. And all who disliked the changes in religion or the men who had made them, rallied round the new Queen in her effort to defeat them. A carefully packed Parliament began to repeal every ecclesiastical act of the last quarter of a century. Orders came down thick and fast upon Winch and his wardens. The use of the Prayer Book was forbidden and the Latin services restored. The Communion Table must be destroyed and the stone altar rebuilt. A new set of vestments must be bought; a crucifix at least five feet high must be set on the rood-loft; lamps, candlesticks, holy water stoups, tabernacles, all must be reinstated. The cup must be withheld from the laity. All married clergy must be expelled from their livings. The climax came on that dark November afternoon (1554), when the Houses of Parliament knelt before the red-robed Papal Legate, and in the name of the whole realm declared themselves "very sorry and repentant" for their schism and sin, and received absolution on condition that they repealed every law "against the supreme authority of the Pope's Holiness."

But the Reformation was not yet undone. Some of the Protestants fled abroad, but the leaders stood their ground, and Cranmer issued a courageous challenge:

The Reign of Terror

"If the Queen will give me leave, I shall be ready to prove against all that will say the contrary that the Communion Book set forth by King Edward is conformable to the order which our Saviour observed and commanded, and that the Mass in many things has no foundation of Christ, the Apostles, or the Primitive Church, but is manifest contrary to the same and contains many horrible blasphemies." It was clear that if Protestantism was to be suppressed it must be stamped out by force. News came that the Archbishop and many others had been arrested (1553); that the old acts against the Lollards had been revived (1554). Then Durford began to hear stories of the martyrs: how Prebendary Rogers, editor of the Bible, had died at Smithfield (4 Feb., 1555), "bathing his hands in the flame, as if it was cold water"; how Prebendary Saunders had been burnt at Coventry (8 Feb.) for preaching in defence of the Prayer Book; how Bishop Hooper had stood in a slow fire in front of his cathedral at Gloucester for three quarters of an hour before death released him (9 Feb.), with a pardon lying on a stool before his eyes, which he could have claimed at any moment, if he had been willing to recant; how Taylor, a typical country parson, burly, fearless, and humorous, had been burnt (9 Feb.) in his Suffolk parish amid the tears of his parishioners. Next month men told how bravely Bishop Ferrar had borne himself at his burning at Carmarthen; how John Laurence had died at Colchester; how laymen were proving as staunch as the clergy; how a barber, a butcher, a weaver, a prentice boy, two Essex gentlemen, and an old Welsh fisherman had laid down their lives for the faith. But it was not till fires were flaming in Canterbury market-place that Durford people really realized what it meant. In July, John Bland, the stout-hearted Rector of Adisham, who had refused to lay aside the Prayer Book at the accession of Mary, and John Frankesh, Vicar of Rolvenden, were burned there with two laymen. In August six laymen died on the same spot. In September five perished in the flames; in October three more. Their quiet courage filled even their enemies with amazement. Men began to see that these Protestants had a faith worth dying for. Men began to ask whence came this power of meeting cruel torture with a smile and song. From other parts of England reports of the same kind came. The dying words of Bishop Latimer passed from mouth to mouth, "Be of good cheer, Master Ridley, we shall this day light such a candle by God's grace, as I trust shall never be put out." Never did Protestantism win converts more rapidly than during this persecution.

Death of Cranmer

In January, 1556, five more martyrs died in Canterbury, "who, when the fire was flaming about their ears, did sing psalms," and this time four of the number were women. Durford Protestants were thanking God for the valour of their champions; but next month they were filled with shame and mortification. The sad, incredible news came that the leader had deserted the colours; Archbishop Cranmer had denied the faith. Worn out physically and mentally by his long imprisonment, badgered daily by Spanish friars, deprived of the books that he needed in order to meet their arguments, at last the old man utterly broken down, and the recantation that he signed was circulated broadcast. But fortunately his enemies were not content with this. He must apostatize publicly in the University Church at Oxford. The preacher ended his sermon with the words, "Brethren, lest any man doubt this man's conversion and repentance, you shall hear him speak." And then Cranmer's courage returned. He boldly denounced the paper he had signed, declaring it "troubleth my conscience more than any other thing that ever I did." "And forasmuch as my hand offended in writing contrary to my heart, therefore, if I come to the fire, it shall be first burned." And he was true to his word. When they rushed upon him, and hurried him to the stake, he held his hand unflinchingly in the flames, till it was consumed. Like Samson, he recovered his strength in the hour of his death; and in that hour did more harm to his enemies than in all the victories of his life.

End of the Persecution

But this was only a passing incident in the wholesale butchery. The unhappy Queen, disappointed in her hope of an heir, who should wrest the throne from Anne Boleyn's daughter, was ever urging on the bishops by her "rattling letters". During the summer (1556) we have details of more than seventy burnings. In one horrible case, the story of which was told far and wide, a woman gave birth to a child in the flames, and the baby, though rescued for the moment, was flung back into the fire and burned.[1] Nor were those who went to the stake by any means the greatest sufferers. Terrible were the tortures of those who remained in the crowded and pestilent prisons. In Canterbury Castle this year four persons died of starvation, unable to keep body and soul together on three farthings a day. All through the following year (1557) the awful carnage continued. Three times the fires were lighted in Canterbury. Other Kentish towns, Wye, Maidstone, Ashford, Rochester, began to have burnings also. 1558 came, and still there was no respite, but now the end was near. On 10 November five more martyrs died at Canterbury, and one of them, a girl named Alice Snoth, sent for her godparents that they might see how true she was to her baptismal vows. These were the last who perished. Six

[1] Foxe has been accused of inventing this story, but every detail can be verified from the State Papers.

days later Mary was dead, and "all the churches did ring, and at night men did make bonfires, and set tables in the street, and did eat and drink, and made merry."

Accession of Elizabeth

Seven years before, Mary had found English Protestants a small and unpopular minority. When she died, they seemed to have won the sympathies of almost the whole nation. Sermons from the stake had been far more convincing than sermons from the pulpit. The sight of neighbours dying for their faith upon the village green had touched hearts that were deaf to all mere exhortation. On Midsummer Day (1559) the English Prayer Book was once more legal. The new edition as printed was practically the same as the Second Book of Edward VI, except for four alterations, meant to conciliate those who clung to the older ways. The prayer for deliverance from the "enormities" of the Pope was dropped out of the Litany. The "black rubric" at the end of the Communion Service was omitted.[1] When the bread and wine were given to communicants the words of the First and Second Prayer Books were combined as in our present service.[2] And the mysterious Ornaments Rubric made its appearance, although it had not been in the book when it was passed by Parliament, directing the minister to "use such ornaments in the church as were in use by authority of Parliament in the second year of the reign of Edward VI." This is not the place to discuss the problems raised by this famous rubric. It is enough to say that it seemed to retain for a time the pre-Reformation ornaments.[3]

[1] Technically this was not an omission, for the Black Rubric was never a part of the *Statutory* Book of 1552, which this Act of Uniformity restored.
[2] First Prayer Book: "The body of our Lorde Jesus Christe, which was given for thee, preserve thy body and soule unto everlasting lyfe". Second Prayer Book: "Take and eate this, in remembrance that Christ dyed for thee, and feede on him in thy hearte by faythe with thanksgiving".
[3] See note at end of chapter.

The Popish Peltry

But this caution proved quite unnecessary. The English Prayer Book was welcomed with enthusiasm. "St. John Baptist's Day," men sang, "Put the Pope away!" The temper of the country proved to be such that in a few weeks the Government changed their policy, and the Royal visitors were encouraging the people to remove the very ornaments which the rubric ordered to be retained. The Churchwardens' Returns give us a vivid picture of what was happening. From those of other places it is easy to construct the kind of report that the wardens of Durford would send in:

"Imprimis, the Roode, Marie and Johnne and all other popishe images were burnte in the presence of the whole parishioners in the firste year of Elizabeth.

"Item, the roode-lofte was pulled downe and formes made thereof.

"Item, the masse-bookes, grailes, legendes and all such peltrei of the pope's sinful service were torne in peces and defaced at the same tyme.

"Item, 2 copes, 2 vestments, 3 amices, 3 stoles, 2 banner clothes were solde, and put to prophane use, and the money put in poore men's box.

"Item, one albe is now put forthe to make our priste a surplice of.

"Item, 1 pax, 1 pyx, 1 sacring bell, 1 crosse, 2 crewets, 2 censers, 14 candlesticks, with other mettell of papistry was broken and solde to a pewterere.

"Item, 1 sepulker and 1 holiwater stock was broken in peces by the handes of the churchwardens."

Results

The Reformation was now an accomplished fact. What had it effected? In the first place much that was false had been swept away. The authority which the Pope had usurped and so grossly abused was abolished. The monastic system had been judged and declared a failure. Three misbeliefs of the middle ages had been exposed and refuted, the doctrine of invocation of saints with all the system of relics and pilgrimages that had clustered round it, the doctrine of purgatory with its chantries and masses for the dead, the doctrine of transubstantiation and all the ceremonies with which it had obscured the meaning of the Holy Communion. But the Reformation did far more than sweep away the false. It conferred upon the country great positive blessings; an open Bible in every parish, which men were encouraged to study for themselves; an English service in every church, which the poorest labourer could take part in; an open road to the throne of grace, the knowledge that justification is by faith alone, and that every one may go straight to the Lord for pardon without waiting for pope or priest or compulsory confession. But one thing it did not do. It did not abolish one Church to set up another. At Durford the same group of villagers worshipped in the same building under the same vicar as part of the same National Church from Henry VIII to Elizabeth. They changed their service books occasionally; first they were in Latin, then in English, then once more in Latin, then again in English. Certain ornaments in the church were removed, then restored, then once more abolished. Certain superstitious practices were discontinued. But there never was a moment, during all those years of change, when the ancient Church itself was abolished and a new one created. The Church of Elizabeth was the same church as the Church of Anselm and the Church of Dunstan, with the same orders, the same creeds, the same two great sacraments, but with "her face washed and dried with a rough towel".

NOTE ON THE ORNAMENTS RUBRIC

The problem of the Ornaments Rubric is a very puzzling one. The *First* Prayer Book of Edward VI retained certain of the pre-Reformation vestments. The *Second* Prayer Book declared that "the Minister shall use neither alb, vestment, or cope, but being a Priest or Deacon he shall wear a surplice only". The Elizabethan Act of Uniformity (1559) restored the *Second* Prayer Book with certain specified alterations "*and none other or otherwise*", yet by a later clause it provided "that such ornaments of the Church and of the Ministers shall be retained and be in use as was in this Church of England by authority of Parliament in the second year of Edward VI (apparently meaning those of the *First* Prayer Book), until other order shall be therein taken by the authority of the Queen's Majesty". When the Elizabethan Prayer Book appeared in print a few months later, it contained an Ornaments Rubric, based on this clause, which had not been in the Book when it was passed by Parliament, ordering the Minister to "use such ornaments in the Church as were in use by authority of Parliament in the second year of Edward VI". Yet all the authorities in Church and State proceeded to act as though the clause and rubric ordered the vestment of the *Second* Prayer Book (i.e., the surplice) and not the vestments of the *First* Book. The Queen's Injunctions, issued the same year (1559) ordered the clergy to wear "both in Church and without" "such seemly garments as were most commonly received in the *latter* year of Edward VI". During the Visitation which followed there was a wholesale destruction of pre-Reformation Ornaments. The Advertisements of 1566 ordered "a comely surplice with sleeves" to be worn by "every minister saying any public prayers or ministering the Sacraments", except in Cathedrals. How can we explain the mystery of Queen and Bishops apparently acting in flat and persistent opposition to the Law and Rubric which they themselves had issued?

Various suggestions have been offered:

(1) There is some evidence that under the First Prayer Book the celebrant changed his vestments, using the Mass vestments for the first part, which was to some extent the Canon of the Mass translated into English, and then putting on the surplice for the Administration of the Holy Communion to the people. In this case the Elizabethan rubric may have taken for granted that the Mass vestments were abolished with the Mass; and in ordering the ornaments in use in the second year of King Edward, have meant the surplice, which was the Edwardian vestment for the actual Holy Communion.

(2) The words of the Proviso at the end of the Act "shall be retained and be in use" may be the equivalent of "held in use", i.e., held in trust, not used, but kept safely and not destroyed until further instructions. In this case the Proviso would be simply a safeguard against embezzlement, and the person, whoever he may have been, who without any legal authority substituted this rubric for that of the Second Prayer Book, which the Act of Uniformity had authorized, either wilfully or accidentally misunderstood the meaning of the phrase in the Act.

(3) The clause and rubric may reflect a temporary fit of timidity on the part of the Queen and her advisers, who may have hoped by

retaining the old vestments to conciliate some of those who had welcomed their restoration under Mary. This, however, was quickly seen to be unnecessary, and the "other order" mentioned in the Act was taken either by the Official Visitors under the Royal Commission or by the Injunctions or by the Advertisements.

Chapter 9

How the Church of England had to fight for its life against Rome and Geneva

An Elizabethan Parish

BEFORE Elizabeth had been many years on the throne Robert Wyborn succeeded Winch as Vicar of Durford. He was a Calvinist, for practically all the younger men had now fallen beneath the spell of the great thinker of Geneva: but he was at the same time a sound and loyal Churchman, believing Episcopacy to be for the good of the Church, believing the Prayer Book to be as helpful and Scriptural a manual of devotion as was likely to be compiled in this imperfect world, willing to obey its rubrics, and seeing nothing in it inconsistent with his Calvinian theology. Every Sunday, Morning Service began at eight o'clock, and the church was full, for a twelve-penny fine was imposed on absentees. All had to sit in their proper seats, according to their rank, according to their sex, according as they were married or unmarried. Sometimes scandals arose through husband and wife, or mother and daughter trying to sit together, and the Archdeacon's Court had to deal with offenders like Abigail Hayward, who "being a yonge mayde sat in the pewe with her mother to the greate offence of many reverend women". Service consisted of Morning Prayer, Litany, and the Ante-Communion, after which Wyborn had to read "gravely and aptly without any glossing of the same or any additions" one of the Homilies set forth by authority. Durford labourers could hardly be expected to comprehend all the parade of learning in those wonderful discourses – "Epiphanius, Bishop of Salamene in Cyprus, writeth thus"; "Lactantius, an old and learned writer, hath these words"; "St. Augustine, the best learned of ancient doctors, saith" – but they would at least carry away the impression that the early Fathers were all on the side of the Elizabethan Settlement. Once a quarter, in obedience to the Archbishop's Advertisements, Wyborn had to compose and preach a sermon of his own, an event looked forward to with considerable excitement in the village. Other things helped to add an interest to the service. From the pulpit a man heard all the business of the little community; whose beasts had strayed; whose turn it was to send wain and men to repair the high road; who had been excommunicated, and who received back to Communion. One heard, too, news of things far outside the village. Special prayers were constantly introduced with little exhortations: "Forasmuch as the Isle of Malta is invaded with a great navy of Turks, it is our parts to assist with hearty and fervent prayer." "Whereas the Turks do now invade the Kingdom of Hungary, it is our parts to assist with spiritual aid." Durford learnt that an army had been sent to help the Huguenots through the prayer for "those which be sent over the Seas to the aid of such as be persecuted for Thy Holy Name". It learnt that another conspiracy had been detected through the prayer "We thank Thee that Thou hast revealed and made frustrate his bloody and most barbarous treason, who hath secretly sought to shed our Queen's blood." Every week the service would provide the village with many topics for discussion under the old yew tree in the churchyard outside. On the first Sunday of every month morning service was followed by the Holy Communion. The Lord's Table was brought from the east end into the body of the church, and the people received the Communion kneeling in their pews. At noon Wyborn was back in church for two hours' catechizing, and all young people under twenty, and such of their elders as could not say the Catechism correctly from beginning to end, had to attend. At two o'clock came Evening Prayer, and again the twelve-penny fine secured a full attendance. At this service also many things happened of great interest to the village: there was no homily, but, after the second lesson, Crump the ploughman brought his youngest daughter to be christened, and there was the excitement of seeing whether the three sponsors satisfied Wyborn and his wardens in their knowledge of the Catechism, for, unless one knew the Catechism, one could not be accepted as a godparent. At the close of the service poor Margaret Tyler had to "stande before ye minister's Reading Desk appareld in a white sheet from head to foot, and in ye presence of ye congregation make her confession as follows: Good People, I confess I have grievously offended Almighty God by falling into foul sin, and thereby given an evil example to my neighbours, for which I am most heartyly sorry, and do earnestly beg pardon of Almighty God and of all others that I have offended by my evil example, and I do promise, by ye grace of God, never to offend in ye like again. And that I may perform my vows and promises I do most earnestly desire your prayers."

Nor was Sunday the only day when the village met at church. There were twenty-two Holy Days in the Elizabethan Calendar, when all parishioners must "withdraw themselves from all worldly and fleshly business," and attend Morning and Evening Prayer under pain of that twelve-penny fine. No work might be done on a Holy Day, except in harvest time, when work might begin at the close of the afternoon service. Every Wednesday and Friday the Litany was said, and a congregation provided by the rule that "every householder dwelling within half a mile of the church" must "send one at least of his household fit to join with the minister in prayers". And every morning and evening Wyborn rang the church bell to invite the parish to join him in worship.

The Churchwardens

Thomas Tilman and Robert Bowlder, the two churchwardens, were persons of great importance in the little community. They had to keep the church in repair, to see that the people attended, and that they behaved reverently when they were present. With white wands in their hands they had to suppress all who "jangle, babble and talk in service time". "They shall first gently admonish them and, if they will not be reformed, they shall lead them up into the chancel door, and set them with their faces looking down towards the people for the space of one quarter of an hour." "If any resort to the ale-house either before service or in time of divine service, they shall bring them to the church and set them at the chancel door as aforesaid." If any proved too stubborn for amendment, twice a year the wardens had to summon them before the Archdeacon at Sandwich. A glance at a typical list of offenders will show how varied were a churchwarden's responsibilities at this time:

"Robert Terry for profaning the Sabbath day by catching eels.

"Jack Gee for disordering himself by excessive drinking.

"Mary Cocke for a great sower of discord and slander in the parish.

"Richard Court for coming unreverently unto the church, never moving his hat till he cometh to his seat.

"Goodwife Swane for that she is vehemently suspected to be a witch.

"Robert Brown for misstopping up our usual way on going the perambulation of our parish.

"Willian Collins for practising surgery without a license.

"Thomas Giles for not sending his servant to be catechised.

"Alice, wife of Thomas Crathorne, for a brawling scold.

"Nicholas Porte, for that he went to plough on St. Matthias Day last."

An Early Puritan

But all villages were not like Durford. In the neighbouring parish of Monksland there was a Calvinist of a very different type. Here Nehemiah Peke was Squire and

Patron of the living, a man in whom Queen Mary's fires had kindled a bitter hatred of everything, however harmless, that Rome had touched or handled. He secured as Vicar, Samuel Dowker, one of the returned exiles, who had fled abroad during the burnings, as hundreds of Englishmen had done, and made his way to Geneva, the city of Calvin. Here he had seen the impressive sight of a city dominated by a church, a civil government whose chief ambition was to bring the lives of the people up to the standard proclaimed by the preachers from the pulpit. In comparison with this, how feeble and unsatisfactory seemed all the compromises of the Elizabethan Settlement! As Dowker, and many clergy like him, returned to English parishes, Geneva was the ideal that they set before them; "that we may altogether teach and practise that true knowledge of God's Word, which we have learned in our banishment and by God's merciful providence seen in the best other Reformed Churches". To them the Prayer Book services seemed nothing but "cloaked papistry and mingle-mangle". They detested especially the surplice and the attitude of kneeling to receive the Holy Communion. "Why," they asked, "should we borrow anything from Popery? Why should we not agree in rites as well as doctrine with the Reformed Churches?" But even more earnestly did they desire the establishment of Genevan discipline. "Doctrine without discipline is like a body without a backbone." If England was a Christian nation, then all English life, public and private, must be made to bow to the laws of Scripture as interpreted by the Church. If we had visited Monksland on a Sunday morning, we should probably have discovered Dowker conducting a service of his own devising, consisting mainly of metrical Psalms, extemporary prayer, and a very lengthy sermon. Perhaps he had hurried through Morning Prayer as a legal requirement, before the congregation arrived, but for all practical purposes the Prayer Book was ignored. One little pecularity of his, which left a lasting mark upon the village life, was his refusal to christen children by names that were not edifying, and the parish became full of little Hephzibahs, Mehetabels, and Nahums, to say nothing of such compound names as Hold the truth, Fight against sin, Know God, Faint not, and Be Faithful.

But Matthew Parker, Elizabeth's first Archbishop, shy, gentle student though he was, was the last man in the world to tolerate anarchy. "Execution," he wrote, "execution of laws and orders must be the first and last part of good government." In 1565 he took the drastic step of cancelling the licences of all the clergy in his diocese. If Dowker wished to continue Vicar of Monksland, he must apply for a new licence, paying "iiij pens for the parchment and the waxe," and this licence would only be issued on condition that he would conform exactly to all the requirements of the Prayer Book, and would wear at all public services the surplice, and in the street the square cap and long gown which were the required clerical dress. Very grudgingly and reluctantly at last the promise was given, but with the firm determination never to rest, till these "dregs of Antichrist" were purged out of the Church, and all things done in England as they were in Geneva.

A Popish Recusant

Meanwhile there was a third type of religion in the villages. At Durford Manor the De Quetivels held fast to the old rites. In the great central chimney a secret chamber was prepared, with an entrance through a sliding panel at the back of a big wardrobe, in which a priest could be hidden, whenever one was able to visit them: and often in the early morning, before the village was astir, Mass was celebrated in the rush-strewn dining-hall. In addition to this, like most of the Roman sympathizers, they occasionally sat through a service in their parish church, believing that they could do so with a clear conscience, for "the Prayer Book," wrote the Spanish ambassador, "contains neither impiety nor false doctrine. The prayers themselves are those of the Catholic Church." But in 1562 William

Allen landed in England "to enforce by many arguments that so great was the atrocity of this crime, that whosoever was contaminated could on no account remain in the Catholic communion." This grave, dignified, handsome young man, who had been Principal of St. Mary Hall, Oxford, was leader of the Roman party all through Elizabeth's reign, and in his great ability and his dogged determination never to yield the smallest point, it must be added, in his utter unscrupulousness also, he was almost a personification of the papal policy. His first act was to bring every Romanist out of the National Church, and to form them into a separate sect.

The Puritan Attack

Here then was the great question which no one could answer: Which of these three types of religion would in the end prevail – the Elizabethen settlement, the Calvinism of Geneva, or the unbending mediaevalism of Rome? Obviously the Church of England would have to fight for its life. On either side it was assailed by earnest and devoted men, who were determined to do their very utmost to destroy it. Let us watch first the Puritan attack. Its leader was Thomas Cartwright, who often slept a night at Monksland on his frequent journeys to the Continent. This ex-Professor of Divinity at Cambridge was undoubtedly one of the most learned men of the age; of his earnestness and sincerity there can be no question; but he was hard, narrow, intolerant as any Spanish inquisitor, pleading for a revival of the Mosaic Law that all false teachers should be stoned. "If this be bloody and extreme, I am content to be so counted with the Holy Ghost." The point of view of his party can be gathered from the literature which he left behind him on his visits. First came the "Admonition to Parliament" (1572), written to show the reader the "true platform of a Church Reformed," so that he may "behold the great unlikeness betwixt it and this our English Church," and "learn with perfect hatred to detest the one and with singular love to embrace and careful endeavour to plant the other." "We in England are so far off from having a Church rightly reformed, according to the prescript of God's Word, that as yet we are scarce come to the outward face of the same." This fierce little pamphlet vigorously demanded the abolition of the Prayer Book, a thing "culled and picked out of that popish dung-hill, the Mass book." In the Primitive Church "ministers were not tied to any form of prayer invented by man, but as the Spirit moved them, so they poured forth hearty supplications to the Lord." Surplices must be abolished, "garments of Balaamites, of popish priests: they keep the memory of Egypt still among us: therefore can no pretence of order make them in any wise tolerable." And the whole system of Church government must be reorganized. "Take away the lordship, the loitering, the pomp, the idleness of Bishops." Restore the three ancient orders of Ministers, Elders, and Deacons. "To these three jointly is the whole rule of the Church to be committed." Ministers must be called by the congregation, and then "admitted to their function by laying on of hands of the company of the eldership only." "Is a Reformation good for France? And can it be evil for England? Is discipline meet for Scotland? And is it unprofitable for this realm? Surely God hath set these examples before your eyes to encourage you to go forward to a thorough and speedy reformation."

Two years later the group of Puritans who gathered round Peke and Dowker were eagerly studying another volume: "A Full and Plaine Declaration of Ecclesiasticall Discipline owt off the Word of God and off the Declininge off the Churche of England from the Same." This was a scholarly and more systematic presentation of the views of the Admonition. Bishops in the modern sense were to be abolished, though the name might be retained for any minister. The Church must be governed by Presbyteries of ministers and lay elders. The Presbytery would ordain.

The Presbytery would rule. The Presbytery would excommunicate. Every member of the Church would be subject to the discipline of the Presbytery. Contempt for it would be sharply punished by the civil authorities. Even kings were subject to the discipline of the Church.

Secret Organization

Soon Dowker began to take steps to practise what he preached. Peke and his fellow-churchwarden were quietly transformed into Elders. The four Sidesmen were taught to think of themselves and act as Deacons. A Conference, which they called the Classis, was formed of all the Puritan ministers and elders in the neighbourhood, and this was recognized as the only rightful authority over them. If the Archbishop issued an order, it was ignored, until it had been discussed and confirmed by the Classis. Candidates for the ministry were first examined and ordained by the Classis, and then sent to the Archbishop's ordination as a mere formality required by the civil law. In many parts of England the same thing was happening. Beneficed clergy were secretly introducing the full Presbyterian system.

Archbishop Whitgift

For a time this policy had considerable success. Archbishop Parker died in 1575, and Edmund Grindal, his successor, the "gentle shepherd Algrind" of the poet Spenser, though one of the most lovable men, lacked strength to grapple firmly with so difficult a position. In 1583, however, Whitgift became Primate, a born bureaucrat, eager to enforce the established order in every detail and particular. The Queen firmly believed in her "little black husband," as she affectionately called him. He obtained from the Government a new Court of High Commission to deal with the "disordered persons commonly called Puritans". A strict censorship of the Press was established, and no book allowed to be printed until it had been submitted to Whitgift and the Bishop of London. No one was allowed to preach until he had signed a statement that the Prayer Book "contained nothing contrary to the Word of God". And at once a considerable number of clergy were suspended.

Martin Marprelate

The Puritan answer came in a most unexpected form. The Elizabethan public dearly loved a joke; and in 1588 a small, badly printed pamphlet began to pass from hand to hand amid Homeric peals of laughter. It was the first of a series of tracts from a secret printing-press, "compiled for the behoofe and overthrow of the Parsons, Fyckers and Currats, that have learnt their Catechismes and are past grace, by the reverend and worthie Martin Marprelate, gentleman". This mysterious writer, who has never yet been satisfactorily identified, was undoubtedly one of the greatest English satirists. A Puritan, disguised as a stage clown, he rollicked round the Bishops, prodding them in the ribs, addressing the Archbishops as Catercaps and Nuncle, raking together ridiculous stories about them, dragging to light all their mistakes and all their personal failings, no one had ever seen such extraordinary pamphlets before. "Brother Bridges" – this for example is the way he accosts the Dean of Salisbury – "a word with you ere we depart. I pray you where may a man buy such another gelding as you have bestowed upon your good patron, Sir Edward Horsey, for his good worde in helping you to your Deanery? Go to, go to, I perceive that you will proove a goose. Deale closeliar for shame the next time. Must I needs come to the knoledge of these things?" Scurrilous undoubtedly the tracts were, but, it must in fairness be added, far less scurrilous than most of the pamphlet literature of the age. And underneath their quips and quiddities, their impudence and fooling, there lay a deep vein of religious feeling. "I used mirth as a covert, wherein I would bring truth to light. The Lord being the author of both mirth and gravitie, is it not lawful for the truth to use either of these ways?"

The Roman Attack

But we must leave all Monksland laughing at the Marprelate pamphlets, and look back to see what is happening in the Manor House at Durford. If the Puritans despised the Church as only half reformed, the Romanists detested it for being reformed at all. We have seen how, under Allen's influence, they had withdrawn from its services. We must now watch, while they plot to destroy the Church altogether. The first need was literature; and many of the chief controversialists withdrew to Louvain, and from this quiet University city in the Spanish Netherlands poured into England a steady stream of bitter little pamphlets. The next need was missionaries. In 1568 Allen founded the English College at Douai,[1] which drew to its doors scores of students from Oxford and the English Grammar Schools, and sent them home keen young priests, eager, alert, desperate, ready to face rack and gallows to win back England for the Pope. Ten years later the Spanish ambassador wrote to his master: "The number of Catholics increases daily, the instruments being missionaries from the seminary at Douai. A hundred of these have returned in the past year. They travel disguised as lay men, and, young as they are, the fervour with which they throw themselves into their work is admirable." A favourite place to slip ashore was the deserted strip of coast between Deal and Ramsgate, and Durford Manor then made a convenient first hiding-place.

Plots and Conspiracies

All this was fair and honourable, but soon the Romanists stooped to use far more doubtful weapons. If we think of Sir Richard de Quetivel as one who began as a gallant

[1] Douai is now on the French side of the Belgian frontier, but was then included in the Spanish Netherlands.

old English gentleman, doggedly refusing to forsake the faith of his fathers, but degenerated slowly into a traitor, plotting to help Spanish troops to invade his own country, and then even became the accomplice and supporter of assassins, we shall have a picture of what was happening in many an old-fashioned home. The great hope of the Romanists lay in the fact that Elizabeth was unmarried, and could not live for ever, and, when she died, the throne would pass to Mary, Queen of Scots. Then indeed the tables would be turned. If Mary I had chastized Protestants with whips, Mary II would assuredly chastize them with scorpions. Soon the temptation became irresistable to the wilder spirits to try and hasten the death of the heretic Queen. In 1563 came the first plot – "an empty business" the Spanish ambassador called it, but significant of what was to follow for the next twenty-five years. In 1564 it was reported from Rome that "remission of sins to them and their heirs" had been promised to "any cook, brewer, baker, vinter, physician, grocer, surgeon, or any other person who would make away with the Queen". In 1569 came the Northern Rebellion, when the Earls of Westmoreland and Northumberland raised the Banner of the Five Wounds, captured Durham, burnt the Prayer Book, and restored the Mass, but then hesitated, and retreated ignominiously into Scotland. This failure caused the Romanists to turn their thoughts to the task of bringing foreign troops against their own countrymen. In 1570 a group of noblemen wrote to Philip of Spain, offering harbours, supplies, anything, if he would send an army. In the same year Pius V launched his Bull against Elizabeth, declaring that she was excommunicated as an incorrigible heretic, and that, since a Pope possessed authority as "prince over all nations," he "deprived her of all and every dominion, dignity, and privilege," absolved her subjects from their oaths of allegiance, and commanded them "not to dare to obey her, her monitions, commands and laws". Next year a formidable conspiracy was formed, in which a large number of Romanist families were involved. "We ask his Majesty," wrote the Duke of Norfolk to the King of Spain, "for money, arms, ammunition and troops, and especially for some experienced soldier to lead us, we on our part providing a place upon the coast where his army can land, entrench itself, and keep its stores. We can ourselves on the spot provide 20,000 foot and 3,000 horse, besides many others who have pledged themselves to take the field upon our side." But once again Cecil's spies detected the plot in time, and Norfolk lost his head on Tower Hill.

The failure of all these efforts led Allen now to bring a new force into the field. Forty years earlier Loyola had formed the Company of Jesus to be a semi-military body to win the world for Rome.

The Jesuits

Every Jesuit was a picked man, only admitted after long and very strenuous probation. His duty was simply to obey the orders given him by his superior.

> Theirs not to make reply:
> Theirs not to reason why:
> Theirs but to do and die.

"I ought to be like a corpse, which has neither will nor understanding" – such was the ideal which Loyola set before each his followers – "or like a small crucifix, which is turned about at the will of him that holds it, or like a staff in the hands of an old man, who uses it as best may assist or please him." Such was the force which Allen now launched against the Church of England. In June, 1580, a soldier "in a suit of buff with gold lace with hat and feathers suited to the same" asked for a night's shelter at Durford Manor. It was Robert Parsons, the head of the Jesuit mission. A fortnight later Campian came, disguised as a jewel merchant. Parsons was an adventurer of the true Elizabethan type, a scholar with a style that is a model of clearness, and a cleverness in controversy that is simply amazing, a courtier who could twist the King of Spain round his little finger, and defeat the wiliest intriguers of the Vatican with their own weapons, but above all a fighter, dauntless, reckless, rollicking, delighting in desperate ventures and prodigious exertions. Campian was a man of a different type, quiet, gentle, fascinating, with a wonderful power of winning the affection of younger men and a gift of eloquence that made him one of the greatest of living orators. The presence of men like this in England soon made itself felt. "I ride," wrote Campian, "about some piece of the country every day. The harvest is wonderful great. On horseback I meditate my sermon. When I come to the house, I polish it. Then I talk with such as come to speak with me or hear confessions. In the morning after Mass I preach. They hear with exceeding greediness. Threatening edicts come forth against us daily. Notwithstanding, by good heed, we have passed safely through the most part of the island." At the end of their first year they boasted that they had made 20,000 converts. The Government was now seriously alarmed. Campian was caught at last, and executed as a traitor (1581), because he refused to disavow the Bull of Deposition. An Act passed "to retain the Queen's subjects in their due obedience" made it treason to be reconciled to Rome, and inflicted a fine of £20 a month on all who, like the De Quetivels, refused to attend their parish churches.

Invasion or Assassination

Henceforth the plots become so numerous that it is almost impossible to disentangle them. Allen and Parsons were tireless in their efforts to stir up the French or Spaniards to invade the country. "The English," wrote Allen, "are as a nation unwarlike, inexperienced, and totally unable to resist the attack of veteran soldiers." "In the whole realm there are not more than two fortified towns which could stand a siege of three days." "The Catholics are now much more numerous than they were, and better instructed by our priests' daily exhortations, so that of all the orthodox in the realm there is not one who any longer thinks himself bound in conscience to obey the Queen. Besides we have nearly three hundred priests in various gentlemen's houses, and we are almost daily sending fresh ones, who, when it is necessary, will direct the Catholics' consciences and actions in the matter." This remark is worth noting, since modern writers often assert that the work of the seminary priests was strictly non-political. "The expenses, whatever they are," adds Allen, "will be borne by the goods of the heretics and the false clergy." In 1583 three sets of conspirators were competing for the honour of assassinating Elizabeth. Next year a gentleman of the Queen's Household was to do the deed, and a letter was discovered on him from the Cardinal of Como stating that the Pope approved of his plans and sent his benediction. In 1586 a gay young officer in a blue velvet jerkin came to Durford Manor. It was Father Ballard, another Jesuit, organizing a formidable plot. Six of the Queen's attendants had sworn to stab her as soon as the signal was given; all the Romanists were to rise; the Queen of Scots was to be released from captivity; and a Spanish army was to land on the east coast. But again Walsingham's Secret Service proved too much for the conspirators, and they brought, not only themselves, but the lovely, reckless Queen of Scots to the scaffold.

The Armada

Before she died, she bequeathed her claim upon the English throne to Philip of Spain, who, both on his father's and mother's side, was descended from John of Gaunt, and therefore the representative of the old Lancastrian line; and soon it was known that he was preparing to conquer his new kingdom. The greatest navy ever seen was gathering at Lisbon. Thirty thousand Spanish veterans were mobilized at Dunkirk, ready to slip across to Margate as soon as the fleet arrived. Allen was given a Cardinal's hat, and appointed Archbishop of Canterbury, with authority to reorganise the Church as soon as the country was conquered. Soon the De Quetivels received a copy of his manifesto, "An Admonition to the Nobility and People of England concerning the present wars made for the execution of his Holiness' sentence by the King Catholic of Spain." After calling Elizabeth "an incestuous bastard," "an infamous, deprived, accursed, excommunicate heretic," he proceeded to say, "His Holiness confirms and renews the sentence of his predecessors. He discharges you from your oath of allegiance. He requires you in the bowels of Christ no longer to acknowledge her as your sovereign. And he expects all of you, according to your ability, to hold yourselves ready on the arrival of his Catholic Majesty's forces to join them." In every Romanist family this Admonition caused great searchings of heart. At Durford, Sir Richard de Quetivel was getting an old man now. His son Hugh was growing disgusted with a religion which forced him to be a traitor; and, after a short spell of painful hesitation, his patriotism triumphed, and, when the bonfires flashed the news that the Spanish galleons were sailing up the Channel, he rode with the rest of the Durford men to the camp at Northbone to fight for England and Elizabeth. And when the danger was past, and the great sea-castles of the enemy were flying panic-stricken up the North Sea, Hugh for the first time in his life entered Durford Church, and knelt with his fellow-villagers at the Thanksgiving Service.

The Church's Defence

Meanwhile, through all these years of vehement and ceaseless controversy, Wyborn continued quietly ministering to his flock at Durford. How did he justify to himself, how did he defend to his people, their rejection of both the rival systems, which were seeking so earnestly, so persistently to win their allegiance? In his study two well-thumbed books lay side by side, one so small that he could slip it into his inner pocket, the other with pages almost as large as those of the great Church Bible. The small book was "An Apology or Answere in Defence of the Churche of England." It was anonymous, but every one knew that its author was Bishop Jewel. It sprang from a sermon of his at Paul's Cross (1560) in which he threw down the challenge: "If any learned man of all our adversaries be able to bring any one sufficient sentence out of any old Catholic Doctor or Father, or out of any old General Council, or out of the Holy Scriptures, or any one example of the Primitive Church, whereby it may be clearly and plainly proved, that there was any private mass in the whole world for six hundred years after Christ, or that there was then any Communion ministered unto the people under one kind, or that the people had their Common Prayers in a tongue that they understood not, or that the Bishop of Rome was then called the Head of the Universal Church, or that the people were then taught to believe that Christ's Body is really, substantially, corporally, carnally or naturally in the Sacrament, or"—and he added twenty other points in which the teaching of Rome differed from that of the Church of England—"if any man be able to prove any one of all these articles, I am content to yield unto him, and subscribe." This argument he then developed in his famous "Apologia," published in Latin (1562) that it might be read by theologians throughout Europe, translated into English (1564) with his approval by Lady Bacon. He boldly asserted that the Church of England was the true successor of the Church of the Great Councils and of the Early Fathers. He proved how modern and unscriptural were most of the doctrines and practices on which Rome laid such stress. He maintained that his own Church was no mushroom sect, but the old historic Household of Faith, purged of certain late disfigurements, and returning to its earlier, higher self. "God's holy Gospel, the ancient Bishops, and the Primitive Church do make on our side. We have not left these men, but rather have returned to the Apostles and the old Catholic Fathers."

In Jewel, Wyborn found a satisfying answer to all the tracts and arguments that came from Durford Manor. For answers to the arguments that came from Monksland he turned to the other volume, a treatise "Of the Lawes of Ecclesiastical Polite" (1597) by his neighbour, Richard Hooker, Vicar of Bishopsbourne. In this book, which "first revealed to the nation what English prose might be," he found proved with unanswerable completeness, with a massive dignity of style and a wealth of illustration from classical and mediaeval sources, and a pre-eminently English appeal to common sense, how untenable was the Puritans' claim that "in Scripture there must be of necessity contained a form of Church polity the laws whereof may in no wise be altered," how narrow and impossible was their view of the Church, how reasonable it was to retain the rites and customs of antiquity, whenever they were "generally fit to set forward godliness," how unreasonable were almost all the criticisms which Peke and Dowker were always bringing against the Church and its services. A Church Protestant but still Catholic, reformed but carefully preserving its continuity with the past, purged of error, but treasuring jealously all that was good in antiquity, admitting the duty of private judgement, but yet respecting authority, a Church seeking to reproduce and adapt to modern conditions the life of the early Church in its best and purest days – such was the ideal which Jewel and Hooker opposed to the ideals of Geneva and Rome.

CHAPTER 10

How Geneva gained the mastery

The New Dynasty

A CRITICAL moment came for the Church, when Elizabeth died (1603), and James I rode slowly south to claim the English crown. Rome hoped great things from the son of Mary Stuart, who, in the course of the crooked diplomacy that his soul loved, had more than once promised Philip that he would "turn Catholic." The Puritans hoped still greater from a King, who had been brought up by Presbyterians, and had publicly expressed the opinion that the Scotch Kirk was "the purest in the world," and the Prayer Book service "but an evil said Mass in English." But the shrewd, pedantic, awkward little man soon decided on his course. "A presbytery agreeth as well with monarchy as God and the devil." He would continue the policy of his predecessor. Both sides then fell back on their old line of of action. The Romanists resumed their plots, first the Bye Plot and the Main Plot (1603), then (1604) Gunpowder Treason. The last, with its desperate attempt to destroy at a single blow King, Bishops, Lords, and Commons, thrilled Durford with horror, and the burning of Guy Fawkes became an annual event, which destroyed all chance of the Papal Party winning the sympathy of the village. On the other hand, the Puritans continued their agitation. The Millenary Petition (1603), to which 750 clergy gave their assent, asked among other points that the cross in baptism should be dropped, that the surplice should not be insisted on, that the ring should no longer be a part of the marriage service, though it might be retained as a private token given by husband to wife, and that Confirmation should no longer be confined to bishops. If a parish clergyman could baptize, why should he not confirm? From the Hampton Court Conference, which followed (1604), they got very little encouragement. When the new Prayer Book appeared (1604), it was found to be practically the same as that of Elizabeth, except that the questions and answers on the Sacraments were now added to the Catechism. This book was rigidly enforced. All clergy who refused to conform were deprived of their livings. "I will make them conform," declared the King, "or harry them out of this land." But this did not make the Puritans any less discontented. All Monksland declared that the Prayer Book which they were compelled to use contained "nineteen Popish errors, three points that are doubtful, seven that are untrue, seven that are disorderly, five that are ridiculous, beside many evident contradictions".

The Witch Panic

The most striking feature of village life now was the witch panic. There had been isolated trials for witchcraft all through the Middle Ages, but in 1484 a Bull of Innocent VIII spread a wave of terror on this subject across Europe. The thunders of the Church, however, only helped to advertise the idea, that it was possible for all, who were willing to renounce Christ, and make a deliberate act of self-surrender to the devil, to gain supernatural powers to hurt and destroy their enemies. Thousands of discontented women yielded to this temptation, and honestly believed that they had entered into alliance with Satan. The mania reached England later than other countries, but by the end of Elizabeth's reign the Church was getting alarmed at the spread of this Devil worship in the country. Jewel lamented in one of his sermons that "witches and sorcerers within these few years are marvellously increased," and Archdeacons in their visitations began to ask the question, whether there were any suspected of witchcraft in the parish. In Scotland they had been burning witches for forty years, and for the last ten years King James himself had been the leader of the hunt. Had he not written his "Daemonologie" to refute all sceptics, who were inclined to doubt the grim reality of this danger? His first English Parliament now passed an act making the penalty for witchcraft death, and under this statute it is said that 70,000 people were executed in the next seventy years. At Durford old Mother Rudge had been for years the village herbalist. In her big cauldron she stewed potions for the cure of diseases. And somehow or other she had drifted into the sin of witchcraft. She believed that she had sold her soul to the Devil. She believed that her black cat was a familiar spirit. She had learned the secret of a powerful unguent that produced wild, wicked nightmares, in which she skirled through the sky on a broomstick, and held high festival with the Prince of Darkness at the witches' Sabbath, or worshipped blasphemously in some vast cathedral, while a monstrous, green-eyed goat celebrated the Black Mass. And then Dick the Waggoner's baby died in a fit, before the vicar could reach the cottage to baptize it, and Dick declared the witch had slain it as a sacrifice to her Master, and the poor, half-crazed old crone was weighed against the big Church Bible, and then packed off to Canterbury jail to await her trial and the gallows. A few weeks later all the village was startled by the news that Lizzie Larter, the miller's daughter, had been seized at midnight in the churchyard digging for dead men's teeth – in those days bodies were still buried without coffins – that she boasted that she had renounced her baptism, and made a compact with the Devil; that she showed with brazen pride the wound where the foul fiend sucked her blood. But, though two witches had been caught, still disasters came. Farmer Mather's cow went mad. Stubbard's horse was seized with staggers. A sudden storm removed the roof of the vicar's tithe barn. Every woman in the place was in danger of being denounced as a witch by some spiteful neighbour. But the witch hunt was not a wholesale massacre of harmless and innocent old women. Behind all the ignorant superstition and panic-stricken cruelty of the persecutors lay this amazing outbreak of real Devil worship. A religion, that rejoiced in everything that was foul and evil, was rapidly gaining devotees in almost every village.

The English Bible

In 1611 the first copy of the new Bible reached Durford Vicarage. This was the only permanent result of the Hampton Court Conference. Bishops and Puritans had agreed that a fresh translation was desirable, and the King had taken up the scheme with enthusiasm. Till now there had been three versions of the Scriptures in circulation. The most popular was the Geneva Bible (1560), a translation made by English exiles in Geneva in Queen Mary's reign. Its quarto shape was easier to handle than the big folios that had preceded it; its Roman type was easier to read than the old black letter; its division into chapters and verses made it easier to refer to; and its notes formed a pithy Calvinistic commentary on the text. Moreover it had maps and metrical Psalms and a catechism on Predestination, and a list of the "godlie names" which parents ought to choose for their children, a list which included Kerenhappuch, Vopsi, and Elichoenai. The marginal notes, however, were unpopular with the Bishops, especially the one which identified them with the locusts in the Book of Revelation, and under the leadership of Parker (1568) they issued the Bishop's Bible, a rather hurried revision of Cranmer's Great Bible. They wisely decided "to make no bitter notes nor yet to set down any determination in places of controversy," but they used their margin for quaint little bits of information like this: "Ophir is thought to be the Iland in the west coast of late founde by Christopher Columbo". Then came the Romanists' version, the New Testament issued from Rheims in 1582, the complete Bible from Douai in 1610. Its appearance did not mean that their Church had abandoned her old attitude toward the reading of the Scriptures. The Preface poured scorn on those who would "so abuse the blessed book of Christ" as to place it "in the hands of every husbandman, artificer, prentice," yet confessed that the special state of the country and the circulation of the "prophane" translations of the heretics had made this version necessary; but it warned all that "the holy Scriptures, though truly and Catholikely translated, yet may not be indifferently read of al men, nor of any other than such as have expresse licence therunto". The translation was made from the Latin Vulgate, which the Preface boldly declared to be "better than the Greek text itself in those places where they disagree," and its English remained very nearly Latin. "Beneficience and communication do not forget, for with such hostes God is promerited" was its rendering of the text "To do good and to distribute forget not, for with such sacrifices God is well pleased," and the reader constantly stumbled across such extraordinary words as commessations, coinquination, azymes, potestats, scenopegia. In many places the text was tuned to a very Roman key. The Baptist's cry of "Repent" became a cry of "Doe penance," and "forbidding to marry" became "disallowing the sacrament of marriage". The margin, moreover, was full of fierce little controversial notes: "Putting heretikes to death is not to shead the blood of Saints." "They that communicate with Heretikes shal be damned with them" (a hit at occasional conformists). "Heretikes may by penal lawes be compelled to the Catholike faith." "A Christian man is bounde to burn al Heretikal bookes." "It is not lawful for Catholikes to marry with Heretikes"—varied by queer little bits of unexpected information: e.g. at the death of St. Stephen "one stone hitting the martyr on the elbow rebounded backe to a faithful man that stoode neere, who was by revelation warned to leave it at Ancona in Italie," or again, "A husbandman in Yorkshire called Kitle had the guift to see evil spirits, whereby he often detected and hindered their bad purposes." But now (1611), after six companies of scholars had worked for "twice seven times seventy-two days," they issued the greatest of all the English versions. They did not scorn the labour of their predecessors. "We never thought," they said in their Preface, "that we should neede to make a new Translation, nor yet to make of a bad one a good one, but to make a good one better, or out of many good ones one Principall good one." Even the Douai Latinisms were not entirely rejected: "Confession is made unto salvation" was seen to be an improvement on "to acknowledge maketh a man safe". Yet substantially this translation remained that of Tindale, but with every word sifted and resifted by ninety years of controversy. Every expression that could be challenged had been challenged again and again. The result was a version that won its way by sheer force of merit.[1] All competitors, except that of Douai, gradually dropped out of print, and King James' Bible reigned without a rival, till the appearance of the Revised Version of 1881-5.

An Arminian Vicar

Another important feature of the reign was the rise of a new school of clergy. A little earlier the Dutch Church had tried to compel its ministers to sign the Calvinistic Heidelberg Catechism. Some of them refused to do so, and their leader was Jacob Hermann, whose name was latinized as Arminius. This had been the beginning of a violent controversy, which had split the Dutch Church into two, and it had become the fashion in England to call every one who opposed Calvinism an Arminian. The views of the new school were rather indefinite. When some one was asked what they held, he replied wittily, "the best bishoprics and deaneries in England". But at all events

[1] Though later known as the "Authorized" Version, apparently it never received any royal or ecclesiastical sanction. The Bishops' Bible remained on the Church lecterns. Eight editions of the Bishops' New Testament were issued by the King's printers in the next eight years. The Geneva Bible remained in the homes. At least fifteen new editions appeared in the next thirty years. The only authorization of King James' Bible was its own excellence.

they held two truths which thorough-going Calvinists denied; they believed that Christ died for all, and that man's will is strong enough to resist Grace, and even to fall from it. John Matson, the new vicar of Durford, was a keen Arminian, a disciple of "little Doctor Laud," whose pupil he had been at Oxford. In his vehement revolt against the prevailing Calvinism he came to the village eager to fight, not only extreme Puritans, but all who clung to Elizabethan ways of thought and worship. The result of the work of men of this type appeared in the next reign. In 1625 Charles I succeeded his father. In 1633 he made Laud Archbishop of Canterbury. In 1625 the Church was strong and popular. By 1645 bishops and Prayer Books were alike abolished, and the whole Church system utterly swept away. What was the explanation?

The Sunday Question

Four things combined to cause the Church's grievous downfall. First the Arminians lost the respect of thousands of the most religious people in the country by opposing things which the national conscience recognized to be right. For instance, nothing could be more desirable than the growing feeling in favour of a quieter and more orderly Sunday. In all the villages Sunday had been a day for rioting and revels. Here is one picture drawn for us by a contemporary hand: "All the wild heads choose a Captain, whom they adopt for their King. He chooseth some three score like himself to guard his noble person. Those he investeth with liveries of green and yellow. This done, they tie about their legs twenty or forty bells. In this sort they go into the church, though the Minister be at prayer or preaching, dancing and swinging their handkerchiefs over their heads with such a confused noise, that no one can hear his own voice. The foolish people they stare, they laugh, they mount upon forms and pews. About the church they go again and again, and so forth into the churchyard, wherein they feast and dance all that day and peradventure all that night too." But almost everywhere customs of this kind were fast disappearing, till bishops and clergy set themselves to revive the Sunday revels. Calvinism had identified the Lord's Day with the Jewish Sabbath, and so the Arminians delighted in proving that they were absolutely distinct. A flood of tracts began to appear on "Sunday no Sabbath". In 1633 every incumbent received from Laud and Charles a declaration which he was ordered to read from the pulpit:[1] "Our pleasure is that after the end of Divine Service our good people be not discouraged from any lawful recreation, such as dancing, archery, leaping, vaulting, nor from having of May games, Whitsun ales and Morris dances, and the setting up of May poles and other sports therewith used." Some Puritans refused to read this, and were imprisoned. Others read it, and then immediately read the Fourth Commandment, adding the brief comment: "Beloved, ye have heard the commandment of man, and the commandment of God. Ye know which ye ought to obey." But the Arminians read it with enthusiasm. In their reaction against Calvinistic sternness they were drifting into a dangerous alliance with the careless, disreputable classes of the community, and alienating sober, God-fearing people, who should have been the backbone of the Church.

The Ritual Question

In the second place they irritated the laity by little innovations in ritual. "They have practised and enforced antiquated and obsolete ceremonies" was one of the complaints which the men of Kent sent to the Long Parliament. "He presseth people to observe new gestures in the church." "He dops, ducks, and bows, as though made all of joints." "He cringeth to the Table, when he retireth from it." "When he consecrateth the bread and wyne, he lifteth them up, and maketh obeysance to them

[1] This was a re-issue of a proclamation made by James I (1618) to deal with a local dispute in Lancashire.

three several times." "He turneth his back to the west, when he pronounceth the Creed." "He carrieth children from baptism to the Table to offer them up to God" – this was the kind of cry that was rising from scores of parishes. But the fiercest controversy raged around the position of the Lord's Table. By the canon it should have been kept against the east wall, but for the Communion it might be brought down into the nave. It was, however, a heavy piece of furniture, and in many churches, like Durford, it was left permanently in the middle of the aisle. Here it became a resting-place for hats. Vestry meetings sat around it. Churchwardens wrote their accounts upon it. Late comers sometimes even sat upon it for the sermon. There was much to be said in favour of Laud's new rule, that it must be removed to the east end, and reverently railed in, and that all who wished to communicate must kneel at the rails. But old-fashioned folk, who had never received the Communion anywhere but in their own pews, naturally disliked and distrusted this innovation. The result in Durford and other villages was an absolute deadlock. The vicar refused to come outside the rails. The people refused to go up to them. He threatened to present them before the Archdeacon for withdrawing from Communion. They threatened to indict him at the next assizes for withdrawing the Communion from them. And so the miserable squabble dragged on, causing continual bad blood and bitter feeling.

The Policy of Repression

If Laud's changes in the accustomed ritual irritated the laity, his attempts at coercion absolutely infuriated them. He failed to realize that England was an adult nation now, ready to respond to reason and to skilful leading, but absolutely impossible to drive. His aim, according to his friend Clarendon, was that "the discipline of the Church should be felt as well as spoken of". There were two Lauds; the Laud whom his friends admired, the man of piety and learning, who loved his garden and his music, who revelled in rare books and unique manuscripts, who had rebuilt his college and reformed his university; and Laud as the outside world saw him, a bustling little martinet of the country tradesman class, with a sharp tongue, a dogged will, and a quick and irritable temper. For abstract thought he cared nothing. It was incomprehensible to him that men should get excited over secrets of eternity, which they could not hope to solve. A bishop's first duty, he said, was to enforce regulations. He had purged Oxford of Puritanism by the pressure of college discipline. He thought that the same methods would purge England too. The Star Chamber cropped the ears of unruly laymen. The Court of High Commission muzzled rebellious clergy. His censorship of the Press silenced all opposition literature. No book or pamphlet might be printed anywhere in England, until he had read and approved of its contents. His visitations brought him closely in touch with every parish, and left no irregularity any possible corner to hide in. Every churchwarden had to report to him in writing, "Do any speak against the rites and ceremonies of the Church? Do any read books tending to Puritanism?" All conventicles and private meetings were sternly repressed. How real the persecution was is proved by the fact that in twelve years 20,000 persons fled from England to seek new homes among the unknown forests and savage tribes of America. At last even Kentish ploughboys began to whistle at their work, "Give little Laud to the Devill".

The Doctrine of Divine Right

The fourth cause of the Church's fall was that it made the mistake of identifying itself with one side in politics, and that side the wrong one. This was a time when political feeling was running deep and strong. Great fundamental questions had to be debated and decided. Was the King of England a limited or an absolute ruler? Could he govern without a Parliament? Could he tax without the consent of Parliament? Could he keep his subjects in prison without bringing them to trial? It was fatal at such a time, when the rising tide of constitutionalism was sweeping everything before it, that the clergy should be the chief advocates of the Divine Right of Kings. Durford was treated to many a sermon on the three proof texts – "By Me Kings reign;" "Submit yourselves to the King as supreme;" "They that resist shall receive to themselves damnation." "The most high and sacred order of Kings," so ran the first of Laud's canons, "is of Divine Right, being the ordinance of God Himself." In many an eloquent discourse Matson expounded this doctrine. A true King's eldest son cannot forfeit his right, by any sin, by any incapacity, by any act of deposition. The rightful heir alone is King, though a usurping dynasty may have reigned for a thousand years. Kings, being God's vice-regents, are accountable to God alone. It is sin, sin which ensures damnation, under any circumstances to resist them. But what if a King commands men to sin? Then they must give passive, not active, obedience. They must refrain from doing the act, and meekly accept the punishment which follows such disobedience. "We must patiently suffer what he inflicts on us for such refusal. Remember Christianity is a religion of the Cross." This strange doctrine did not originate among courtier prelates eager to win the favour of the King. It sprang from the struggle with Rome. It sprang from the Church's Protestantism. It was the answer of English theologians to the Pope's claim to depose. "All Kings," wrote Thomas Aquinas, "are subject to the Pope." "No," replied English Churchmen, "the King holds his position directly from God. No matter how he may misgovern, God can control his own viceroy. We must leave him to God to punish." But now the majority of thoughtful laymen had come to believe that the King held his power solely from the choice and consent of his people, and it was maddening to have to hear Sunday after Sunday from the pulpit: "His Majesty is not bound by any laws of this realm.

His royal will may not be resisted without peril of eternal damnation."

The Long Parliament

At last (1640) news came, that Charles had been forced to call a Parliament, and then the long pent-up indignation found expression. Kent chose as its representative Sir Edward Dering, a keen Church reformer and a bitter opponent of Laud; and his first act was to present a great petition from the county, praying that the rule of Bishops "root and branch may be abolished". Similar petitions poured in from other counties also, and curiously enough no one regarded these as attacks on the Church. Dering considered himself rather a strong Churchman. The House of Commons opened its session by receiving the Holy Communion. The idea that anyone could consider Bishops as essential to the Church had not entered the head of any average layman. The petitioners pleaded for the reform of certain practical abuses, and among other things the removal of a small group of officials, who had proved themselves to be a nuisance. As a first step Laud was lodged in the Tower for "subverting the constitution". The Star Chamber and the Court of High Commission were abolished. Then came the task of investigating the grievances of particular parishes. A Committee for Scandalous Ministers was appointed with Dering as its chairman, and, when the turn of Durford came, Matson was removed from the living, "for that he hath refused to administer the Lord's Supper to those that would not come up to the rails, and hath expressed great malignity against Parliament and the proceedings thereof". His successor was Jehoram Benskin, a pronounced Puritan. The new Communion rails were quickly broken up for firewood, and the Lord's Table brought back into the body of the church. But soon the wilder spirits began to get out of hand. News came from Canterbury of the exploits of Blue Dick, who led a mob into the Cathedral, "smashed the great idolatrous

Destruction of Communion Rails.[1]

windows, overthrew the Communion Table, rent the surplices and mangled the Service Books, bestrewing all the pavement with the leaves thereof". Moderate men became alarmed, and large numbers in the county signed a new petition, praying Parliament "both in Church Government and in our present Liturgie to give us a severe Reformation, not an absolute Innovation".

Civil War

Meanwhile the nation was drifting daily nearer war. News came (1642) that the King had fled from London, and raised his standard at Nottingham. Durford farmers began to fall apart into two parties. De Quetivel and his tenants wore in their hats the King's tawny ribbons. Most of the younger yeomen wore the Parliament's orange. But there was not any general rush to arms. In our village, as in other parts of England, the majority remained neutral. "The number of those who desired to sit still was greater than those who wished to engage in either party." The Sandwich carrier brought the news that a Puritan merchant and ten townsmen had scaled the walls of Dover Castle, and captured it at midnight for Parliament. A troop arrived to search the Manor House for arms and ammunition, but De Quetivel with his grooms and huntsmen had already started for the north. The keener Parliamentary enthusiasts also left the village to join the army that was going to "free the King from ill advisers." But no one yet realized what lay ahead. "We all thought," Baxter confessed, "that one battle would decide." Then bit by bit news from the war came back into the village. Everywhere the King seemed to be winning. At Edgehill, Essex had failed to check his advance. Fairfax was being driven from Yorkshire. Waller was crushed in the west (1643). Parliament could not win without help from Scotland, and the Scots demanded, as the price of their help, that England should become Presbyterian. "What hope can there be of unity, till there be one form of ecclesiastical government?" And Parliament gave way. One Sunday (Feb., 1644) a copy of the Solemn League and Covenant was nailed up in Durford Church porch. After the sermon Benskin read it aloud from the pulpit, and then called upon all who were over eighteen to raise their hands and take the oath: "With our hands lifted up to the most high God we swear (1) that we shall endeavour to bring the Churches of God in the three Kingdoms to the nearest conjunction and uniformity in religion; (2) that we shall endeavour the extirpation of popery, prelacy, superstition, heresy, schism, and profaneness." As he left the church everyone had to sign his name or his mark to the roll. Geneva had conquered. But Matson chuckled over the discovery that the Covenant contained 666 words, the number of the Beast.

The New Service Book

Some months earlier Parliament had summoned the Westminster Assembly of 121 "godly and learned divines" "to confer among themselves of such discipline and government as may be most agreeable to God's Holy Word and most apt to procure the peace of the Church at home and nearer agreement with the Church of Scotland and other

Reformed Churches abroad, and touching the Directory of Worship or Liturgy hereafter to be in the Church." In due time (1645) the new "Directory for Publique Worship" reached Durford. The Preface declared that "sad experience hath made it manifest that the Liturgie used in the Church of England hath proved an offence not only to many of the Godly at home, but also to the Reformed Churches abroad." The new book contained no prayers, but simply directions to the minister as to how the service must be conducted, and what subjects he must pray for in his own words. Let us watch a service in Durford Church according to the new model. The church is full, for the fines are still in force. On one side sit the men, with their grey cloaks and knickerbockers and close-cropped hair, all wearing their broad brimmed hats, which they only remove for the prayers. At their feet the big sheep dogs lie quietly curled up, conscious that the dog-whipper's eyes are upon them, and his tongs ready to remove them, if they disturb the service. On the other side sit the women with their aprons and striped petticoats and bunched up skirts, and their hair neatly smoothed away under linen caps. Benskin enters, wearing his hat but neither gown nor surplice, and begins with a solemn prayer "acknowledging the incomprehensible Greatness and Majesty of the Lord and humbly beseeching for Pardon, Assistance, and Acceptance in the whole service". Then comes a lengthy Bible Reading – a Psalm, an Old Testament and a New Testament chapter with expositions. Then the congregation sing one of Rous's "Psalmes in English Meeter,"[1] and, as few can read, Benskin gives out each line before they sing it. Then comes a long and wonderfully comprehensive prayer, acknowledging "first Originall sin, and next Actuall sins, our own sins, the sins of Magistrates, of Ministers, of the whole Nation, and such other sins as the congregation is particularly guilty of," praying for "full assurance of Pardon, for sanctification and strength," for

[1] These are the Metrical Psalms still used in Scotland.

"the Propagation of the Gospell to all Nations; the conversion of the Jews; the fall of Antichrist; the deliverance of the distressed Churches abroad; our Plantations in remote parts of the World; that Church and Kingdom, whereof we are members; for the King's Majesty, that God would save him from evill counsell; the conversion of the Queen; the religious education of the Prince; for the comforting of the afflicted Queen of Bohemia; for the restitution of the Elector Palatine of the Rhene to all his dominions and dignities," and for twenty-nine other subjects all duly scheduled. Then the sermon, an hour long, its progress carefully timed by the running out of sand in the great pulpit hour-glass. Then another prayer giving thanks "for the light and liberty of the Gospell, the Reformation, the Covenant, and many temporal blessings," the Lord's Prayer, another Psalm, and then the Blessing. Anyone using the old Prayer Book, either in public or private, was liable to a five pounds' fine for the first offence, for the third a year's imprisonment. But Matson, who conducted daily service in the hall of the Manor, evaded these penalties by repeating the well-known prayers by heart, and reading Psalms and Epistles and Gospels from the Bible.

Chapter 11

How Geneva lost its opportunity and Rome was finally defeated

The Failure of Presbyterianism

WITH the King's cause everything was going ill. The terrible Cromwell had created a new type of soldier, sober, sturdy, God-fearing; and Rupert's roysterers could not stand against the New Model. Naseby (1645) destroyed the last hope of a Royalist victory, and after ten months of wandering, Charles, "disguised as a groom," took refuge with the Scots. Seven months later (1647) the Scots surrendered their embarrassing guest to Parliament. But the new Presbyterian Church also was in serious difficulties. In more than half the counties of England its elaborate system of classes and synods never got to work. In the parishes its sour intolerance was creating a tyranny more galling than that of Laud, and everywhere men were rebelling against its discipline. To the average pleasure-loving Englishman it seemed to be

> A sect whose chief devotion lies
> In odd perverse antipathies,

and in nothing was this more true than in its grotesque crusade against Christmas. For example, at Canterbury (1647) the Mayor issued the following proclamation: "All persons are to take heed and remember that Christmas Days and all other superstitious festivals are utterly abolished. All ministers and churchwardens are warned that there be no prayers or sermons in the churches on the said 25th December. And whosoever shall hang at his door any holly or other superstitious herb shall be liable to the penalties decreed by last year's ordinance. And whosoever shall make either plum pottage or nativity pies is hereby warned that it is contrary to the said ordinance." In spite of this a secret service was held in St. Andrew's Church, and, when the Mayor interfered, "his heels were slung up, and he was thrown into the kennel". The Grand Jury (1648) refused to bring in a true bill against the rioters, and preparations went rapidly forward for a Royalist rising. An imposter, who landed at Sandwich, declaring that he was the Prince of Wales, was received with transports of joy. Seven thousand men took up arms for the King, but they were powerless against the discipline of the new Army. In one fight at Maidstone the revolt was suppressed. Next year (1649) the "Kingdom's Weekly Intelligencer" brought the news to Durford, that Charles Stuart, "the man of blood," had been condemned to death for having "levied and maintained cruel war against the Kingdom", and that the office of King had been abolished as "unnecessary, burdensome, and dangerous to the liberty of the people". Next Sunday the board with the Royal Arms had vanished from the chancel arch. Then men learned how the hand of Cromwell had crushed the rising in Ireland (1649), had broken the power of the Scots at Dunbar (1650), had utterly defeated the younger Charles' dash into England at Worcester (1651), had dissolved with twenty musketeers the rump of the Long Parliament (1653). The Army could beat down all opposition, but it could not make the new Church popular. Nor did it wish to do so. The sternest critics of Presbyterianism were found among Cromwell's troopers.

The Independents

At Durford interest centred round the doings of Jehu Murch, one of Cromwell's red-coats, whom a bullet from Basing House had forced to retire from the army. He returned to the village to be a sharp thorn in Benskin's side, for, like so many new model soldiers, he was an Independent. To him Presbyterianism was as anti-Christian as Prelacy. Every attempt to think of the Church as a great institution, mapped out into parishes, controlled by Assemblies, entering into close relations with the civil government, seemed the rankest blasphemy. To him a Church was a little company of truly converted persons, meeting in the Name of Christ and claiming His Presence in the midst. "Besides these particular Churches there is not instituted by Christ any Church more extensive or Catholique." Each congregation formed a separate and entirely autonomous Church. To Christ alone it was responsible for its creed, its worship, and its discipline. No neighbouring Church, no Bishop or Assembly, had any right to interfere between a Church and its Master. In the reaction against the rigid pressure of Presbyterian discipline, this new ideal attracted to itself many of the most earnest spirits. And one of the most burning questions of the day was, Could men like Jehu Murch be allowed to hold services, and form Independent Churches, in the midst of Presbyterian parishes? The Presbyterians strongly opposed any toleration. "To let men serve God according to their own consciences is to cast out one devil that seven worse may enter in." But all the best soldiers in the Army were Independents now. Cromwell, Milton, Vane, the three greatest men of the age, inclined to their side. And the same Instrument of Government (1653), which made Cromwell Protector, decreed that "such as profess faith in God by Jesus Christ, though differing from the doctrine or discipline publicly held forth, shall not be restrained from the exercise of their religion, provided that this liberty be not extended to Popery or Prelacy." Henceforth Murch was as free in his barn as Benskin in the parish church.

Civil Marriage

Every day the Presbyterian regime grew more and more unpopular. It seemed heathenish to lay the dead in the grave without a word of prayer, as the Directory ordered to be done. Still more heathenish seemed the abolition of Christian marriage (1653). A young couple might have their banns called "at the close of the morning Exercise in the publique Meeting Place, commonly called the Church," or "in the Market Place on three Market Days," but for their wedding they must join hands before a Justice of the Peace, "and no other marriage shall be held a marriage according to the laws of England." The entry in the Church register simply recorded the event: "The publycations of Obadiah Bourne and Temperance Taylor wear on 14. 21. 28 June published in Sandwich market place, and they wear mairied 16 October by Tobyas Clerk, mayar of Sandwich." How unpopular this was is seen by the fact that even Cromwell's daughters insisted on being married secretly by a clergyman with the forbidden Prayer-Book service.

Religious Chaos

Meanwhile all sorts of strange preachers began to make their appearance, and to seek for converts upon the village green. First a fervent Apostle of the Family of Love, a queer little Dutch sect, with an elaborate hierarchy of various orders of priests, and a very dangerous doctrine of sinless perfection. Next a Fifth Monarchy Man, calling for the abolition of all existing institutions – for did they not spring from William the Conqueror, and was he not the Little Horn denounced in the Book of Daniel? Then a Seeker, declaring that the whole world was apostate, that nowhere could any true Church or ministry or sacraments be found. Then a Ranter urging Durford folk to burn their Bibles as "the cause of all misery and division in civil and religious affairs," declaring that every ivy leaf and every blade of grass was God, calling men to cease to "mind a Christ who died in Jerusalem," but to "eye and mind the Christ in themselves." A Quaker from Deal burst into "the Steeple-house," as he scornfully called the church, and stripped himself naked as a sign to the people of their own spiritual nakedness, and denounced Benskin to his face as a dead dog and a hireling. Every year it became more evident that the Commonwealth had failed. The Puritans had never been more than a minority of the nation, though a noble and high-minded minority, immensely active and persistent, and even the genius of Cromwell could not make them a majority. They had failed to win the sympathy of old-fashioned Church people; they had failed to control the wilder spirits on their own left; they were divided themselves into three camps, Presbyterian, Independent, Baptist. Even the iron will of the great Protector sometimes quailed. "God knows," he cried, "I would have been glad to have lived under my woodside and to have kept a flock of sheep, rather than have undertaken this government." But now the end was near.

The Restoration

On Monday, 30 August, 1658, the day of the great storm, Durford Church was thronged with people wrestling earnestly in prayer. For news had come that Oliver Cromwell was sick unto death, and even those, who had been his critics, trembled to think what would happen when he had passed away. But their prayers were not answered. On Sunday tidings reached the village that Oliver was dead, and that Parliament had proclaimed his son Richard Protector in his stead – poor, sluggish "Tumbledown Dick." But he had not a chance. The Army made his rule impossible, but could not rule itself. The country was drifting into anarchy, and it was clear to all that the only hope of stable government was to recall the King. On 26 May, 1660, Charles landed at Dover, and passed through Durford the same afternoon. Gaily the procession cantered down the village street, while the people cheered, and the church bells rang out a merry peal. There was the King, that tall figure by the side of General Monk, the little fat Presbyterian to whom he owed his throne. There among the courtiers who rode behind, "all ribbon, feather and romanco," the villagers recognized Bryan de Quetivel, the old grey-headed squire, at last come back from his travels. As Benskin stood at the churchyard gate, and looked at the dark, expressionless features of the new King, he tried to divine what this man's return would mean for religion. For nineteen years Benskin had been minister of Durford, and he had done his work faithfully and well. Was he now to be ejected from his living, or could some compromise be found in ceremonies and Church government, by which he and hundreds like him could be included in the National Church? This was what he hoped and expected. There were cases, in Elizabeth's reign and later, of clergy in Presbyterian orders received in Churches abroad, being admitted to English benefices without reordination. The King owed a great debt to the Presbyterians. They, more than anyone else, had made his return possible. Before he landed, he had promised in the Declaration of Breda: "No man shall be disquieted or called in question for differences of opinion in matters of religion," words which the Presbyterians interpreted as a pledge that they should retain their parishes. This was the great question that had now to be settled. Could the Church of England comprehend all that was best in English religious life, or must it be rent asunder by a terrible schism?

The Act of Uniformity

For the moment nothing happened. The Royal Arms freshly painted reappeared on the Chancel arch. Clergy ejected under the Commonwealth were restored to their livings. But John Matson had long been dead, and Benskin remained undisturbed, and continued to use every Sunday the Directory, to which the village had now grown quite accustomed. But very anxiously did he look for all the news from London. It was reported (1661) that the King had appointed twelve Bishops and twelve Presbyterians to meet in conference in the Savoy Palace "to review the Prayer Book, and to make such reasonable alterations therein, as shall be agreed to be needful or expedient." Then came tidings that the Conference had failed, that the

Bishops had stiffly refused to make any real concessions, that Convocation had issued (1662) a new edition of the Prayer Book, and that Parliament had passed a Bill enacting (1) that every "person in possession of any benefice, who is not already in Holy Orders by episcopal ordination," shall "before the Feast of St. Bartholomew be ordained according to the form of episcopal ordination," or else "all his ecclesiastical promotions shall be void, as if he were naturally dead"; (2) that every "minister whatsoever upon some Lord's Day before the Feast of St. Bartholomew shall publicly read Morning and Evening Prayer according to the Book of Common Prayer," and then "publicly declare his unfeigned assent and consent to everything contained or prescribed in the said book"; (3) that "no form of common prayers shall be used in any church than what is prescribed in the said book".

Black Bartholomew

When the news arrived, Benskin saw that only one course was possible. "I cannot," he said, "after being a Presbyter nearly thirty years, declare myself moved by the Holy Ghost to apply for the office of deacon." But for his friend Enoch Barker at Monksland the problem was not so simple. He was already in Episcopal Orders. All would depend on what the new Prayer Book contained. The revision had been very thorough. About six hundred alterations had been made: Obsolete and ambiguous words had been removed. Several beautiful prayers had been added, including Laud's Prayer for Parliament, the Ember collects, the General Thanksgiving, and the Prayer for all sorts and conditions of men. Petitions against rebellion and schism had been added to the Litany. An Office for the baptism of adults appeared for the first time, made necessary "by the growth of Anabaptism through the licentiousness of the late times," useful also "for the baptizing of Natives in our Plantations." But nothing had been done to meet the scruples which Barker felt most strongly; the surplice was retained, and the cross in Baptism, and the attitude of kneeling at Communion, Saints' Days, and wedding-rings, and lessons from the Apocrypha, and Confirmation by Bishops. Little groups on the village green discussed what he would do, and, when the critical Sunday came, every one was in church. As soon as he gave out his text, it was clear what his decision was, "Esteeming the reproach of Christ greater riches than the treasures of Egypt". On Monday morning there was a sale in each vicarage. That afternoon Barker and Benskin started off together to face a new life of poverty in London. All over England the same thing was happening. Probably nearly two thousand ministers left their parishes. The Church lost a large proportion of its most earnest clergy, for it was the best who went out, the careless and indifferent who conformed. It lost all hope of being the Church of the whole nation. A large section of English Christianity henceforth would be outside its borders. And yet it is difficult to see what else could have been done. No form of service could possibly be devised that would satisfy Prayer Book men and men who loathed all Liturgies, and neither Churchmen nor Presbyterians would have considered for a moment the Independent suggestion that every parish should do what seemed right in its own eyes. For the future at any rate the Church's position was unmistakably defined. It was an Episcopal Church, a liturgical Church, a Church which had definite limits, outside which no one could step and remain a member.

Two Types of Restoration Clergy

The filling of two thousand livings was not an easy task. To Monksland came Noah Webb, a conforming Puritan, who had swallowed all his scruples and accepted ordination, the first of a long succession of Latitudinarian vicars, men who had no strong convictions for which they were prepared to make sacrifices. He came prepared to do anything that was necessary to retain his benefice, but he soon found that he could continue many of his old customs. Nothing happened, if he forgot to put on his surplice. No one haled him before the Bishop's Court, if he administered Communion in the pews. No one protested, if he curtailed part of the Prayer Book service to leave more time for a long extempore prayer before the sermon. No cross was ordered to be used in the service for private baptism, and it was easy to make it the custom in the village for babies to be baptized at home. To Durford, on the other hand, came Andrew Foat, a fierce old Cavalier parson, who during the war had thrown off his cassock, and served under Rupert as cornet. His long exile in foreign lands had made him irritable and intolerant. His creed had one single clause, "I believe in the Divine Right of Kings".

The Cult of the King

Just as the Roman Church from time to time throws all its strength into the task of rousing enthusiasm for the cult of some new saint, so men like Foat tried, night and day, to work up a passionate fervour of devotion to the Throne. Two new Red-Letter Days were added to the Prayer-Book Calendar. January 30 was marked KING CHARLES MARTYR, and men were bidden to pray for "grace to provide for our latter end by a careful, studious imitation of this Thy blessed Saint." May 29 was consecrated to KING CHARLES II, NATIVITY AND RESTORATION. Churches were dedicated to King Charles the Martyr in various parts of the country. The old superstition that a king's touch had power to heal scrofula was revived on such a scale, that the days of pilgrimage seemed to have returned. Crowds of sufferers from every county flocked to the King to be cured. The Register of the Chapel Royal alone records the touching of 92,107 persons, and many thousands more were touched in other parts of the kingdom. Durford Churchwardens' Accounts contain a typical entry: "It was ordered that Lovejoy's boy shall be carried to London to be touched for King's Evil at the charge of the parish." The village never tired of listening to the lad's story of how the Vicar's friend had met him at London Bridge, and had taken him to lodgings near Whitehall, how the King's chirurgeon had examined him and given him a ticket for the ceremony, how the yeomen of the guard had marshalled the patients in the great Banqueting Chamber, how the King had entered with a wondrous crowd of clergy, lords and ladies, how a Bishop had read part of the sixteenth chapter of St. Mark's Gospel, and, when he came to the words, "They shall lay their hands on the sick and they shall recover," Lovejoy had been led forward to the steps of the throne, and the King had stroked both his cheeks, and hung round his neck a white silk ribbon with a little gold medal on it. Who could doubt that the King was more than human, since he had the power of working miracles!

The Popish Plot

But soon news of another kind began to come from London. An uncomfortable suspicion spread abroad that, though the struggle with Geneva was over, Rome was still undismayed and planning a new enterprise. More than a hundred and fifty Jesuits were now at work in England, and their Society was never content with the conversion of individuals; it sought to capture by political methods supremacy in the State. And they had much at this time in their favour. Charles was a man utterly devoid of any personal religion, but his knowledge of France had led him to believe that the Roman Church was the most useful Church to a King who wished to be absolute. His Queen was a Romanist. His eldest illegitimate son was a Jesuit priest. His brother James, the heir to the throne was received (1669) into the Roman Church. Of the Cabal of seven who ruled the country, two were Roman Catholics. In 1670 the King secretly pledged his word to Louis XIV to declare himself a Romanist, to enforce Romanism in the English Church, and to crush any resistance with French and Irish soldiers. But his first step, the Declaration of Indulgence (1672), granting freedom of worship to Roman

Catholics and all other Dissenters, roused such a storm of opposition, that he hesitated, withdrew the Declaration (1673), and postponed indefinitely his public conversion. The hopes of the Jesuits now centred round James, and wild talk began to circulate in their seminaries abroad about removing Charles to make room for his brother. Some of this was overheard by that rascal Titus Oates, and one day (1679) Durford was horrified by a pamphlet, which Luke Goldup brought back from Sandwich market, "A True Narrative of the horrid Plot and Conspiracy of the Popish Party against the life of his Sacred Majesty, the Government, and the Protestant Religion." Most of the details were mere inventions of Oates' fertile brain, but the assassination of the magistrate who had taken his deposition, and a packet of letters hidden in a chimney by the Duchess of York's secretary, showed that something dark and dangerous had been going on, and the whole country was seized by a most discreditable panic. Scores of perfectly innocent victims were hurried to the gallows. The green ribbons of Protestantism fluttered from every hat. Night after night the Pope was burnt in effigy. But, through all the tumult, the Jesuits bided their time.

James the Second

It came at last, when James II succeeded to his brother's throne. Then the newspapers brought each week bewildering news to Durford. The King had publicly declared himself a "son of the Society of Jesus." Father Petre, the Jesuit Vice-Provincial, had been made Clerk of the Royal Closet, and given sumptuous apartments at Whitehall, which James himself had occupied. Four Popish Bishops had arrived in England as Vicars Apostolical. The Jesuits had begun to open schools all over the country. The Rector of Putney had become a Romanist, and still retained his benefice. The clergy had been forbidden to preach against the doctrines of Rome. The Court of High Commission had been revived, with Judge Jeffreys as

President, to see that this order was obeyed. The Bishop of London had been suspended for refusing to enforce the order. An ambassador had gone to Rome to obtain the Pope's permission for Father Petre to be made Archbishop of York. Two Oxford colleges had been turned into Popish seminaries. Then all the fellows of Magdalen had been turned adrift to make room for Roman successors with the Bishop of Madaura as President. A great camp had been formed on Hounslow Heath to overawe London. The army was being filled with Roman Catholic officers. It seemed as though the days of Mary were going to return.

The French Refugees

Just at this critical time there came across the Channel tidings of how Louis XIV was treating his Protestant subjects. He had quartered dragoons on all their houses with orders to convert them by force. "There is no wickedness or horror which they did not put in practice to force them to change their religion. They hung men and women by the hair or feet on the chimney hooks, and smoked them with wisps of wet hay, till they were no longer able to bear it; and, when they had taken them down, if they would not sign, they hung them up immediately again. They tied ropes under their arms and plunged them into wells, from whence they would not take them, till they had promised to change their religion. They stripped them naked, and stuck them with pins from the top to the bottom. With red-hot pincers they took them by the nose, and dragged them about their rooms, till they promised to be Catholics. They held them from sleeping seven or eight days, relieving one another day and night to keep them waking." Then (1685) the Edict of Nantes, by which Louis' grandfather had granted freedom of worship to the Huguenots, was revoked. All Protestant places of worship were razed to the ground. All Protestant services of any kind were forbidden. All children of Protestant families were baptized by a priest, and torn away from their parents to be brought up in convents. Any attempt to leave the kingdom was punished by sentence to the galleys. Yet, in spite of the way the coast was watched, thousands of refugees began to pour into Kent, some hidden in wine casks, some beneath bales of cloth, some making their way across the Strait in open boats, and in Dover, Sandwich, Canterbury, Maidstone, they received the warmest welcome. All England was ringing with the story of their sufferings. A Brief authorized every parish to make a collection to relieve them, and this produced the remarkable sum of £63,000. And as every market-day Durford men brought home fresh stories of torture perpetrated by the French King and his Jesuits, they said to one another, Our King too is a tool of fanatical Jesuits; our King too has declared his desire to convert every Protestant in his realm. Is this what he is planning for us?

The Seven Bishops

The one hope left to Englishmen lay in the fact that James had no son, and both his daughters were Protestants. Indeed Mary, his heir, was the wife of the champion of Protestantism in Europe, William, Prince of Orange. Whatever James did would be undone, when Mary came to the throne. But soon even this hope became uncertain. For Jasper Webb, Vicar of Durford, received a Form of Thanksgiving, which he was ordered to use in church, praising God for His goodness in giving the Queen the hope of bearing a child. If the unborn infant should prove to be a boy, then indeed the Jesuits would triumph. For he would be their pupil, and the future King. Even those who had been the firmest believers in Divine Right began to feel that duty demanded something sterner than passive obedience. A few months later (1688), Jasper Webb had to make his decision. A Declaration arrived from the King, which he was ordered to read aloud from the pulpit. In this James declared: "We heartily wish that all the people of our dominions were members of the Catholic

Church," and announced that, "by virtue of our Royal Prerogative," he had suspended all laws against Romanists and other Dissenters. What would Webb do? In those days of slow communication there was hardly any chance of concerted action. At the best he would only be able to take counsel with a few of his nearest neighbours. The King's mood was arbitrary. The Ecclesiastical Commission was as summary as a court martial. To refuse to read meant almost certainly to be ejected from his living, and to be declared incapable of holding any other preferment. Yet he disobeyed. James had made even such a man as Jasper Webb a rebel. And then he learned that practically all the clergy had done the same; that Archbishop Sancroft and six other Bishops had ventured to petition the King against the Declaration, "because it is founded on such a dispensing power as hath been often declared illegal in Parliament"; that James had clapped all seven into the Tower on the charge of issuing a false, seditious, and malicious libel against him; that they had gone to prison through lanes of kneeling men and women, who begged for their benediction and kissed their robes. Then Durford waited anxiously for the result of their trial, and the night that the squire's groom brought the news that the verdict was not guilty, there was the biggest bonfire on the green that the oldest inhabitant could remember, and from every village round you could hear the church bells ringing.

The Revolution

But there was another piece of news, and this was far more serious. The Queen's child had been born, and it was a boy! The nation flatly refused to believe that such a calamity could have happened. A sentence in a Jesuit manual was unearthed or invented, which declared it lawful, when the good of the Church required, to practise pious fraud and bring forward an imaginary heir. The wildest tales gained credence. The boy was not born of the Queen at all, but a miller's brat smuggled into the Royal bed in a warming-pan. The King had stooped to common trickery to keep his daughter from the throne. This was false, but the next piece of news was true. The King had commanded the Archdeacons to send to Judge Jeffreys the names of all clergy, who had failed to read the Declaration. In thousands of quiet country vicarages clergy began to consider whether they had rightly interpreted the doctrine of Passive Obedience. "True," they said, "St. Paul taught that Christians must not rebel, even against Nero. But suppose somebody else rebelled, suppose the Senate and the Legions rose to hurl him from his throne, St. Paul never enjoined Churchmen to fly to arms in his support. We may not resist King James," they argued, "but if the Whigs resist him, we are not bound to rescue him." And the Whigs were already acting. The rumour spread that an invitation had been sent to William of Orange the son of James' elder sister, and husband of James' daughter; that he was coming to call a free Parliament, which would decide what steps should be taken to preserve English liberty and the Protestant Religion; that the Bishops had refused the King's command to sign a Declaration of Abhorrence of his coming. One afternoon a breathless courier galloped through Durford with tidings that William's fleet was passing Dover and sailing westward. Five weeks later all was over. The bloodless Revolution was accomplished. William was in Whitehall. James had fled to France. The Jesuits had played their last card, and been beaten.

Chapter 12
How the Church went to sleep

The Non-Jurors

THE Revolution was over. The majority of the nation had accepted William and Mary as King and Queen. And now (1689) "all ecclesiastical persons," from the Primate to the humblest curate, from the heads of the Universities to the master of the poorest grammar school, were required to take the oath of allegiance to the new sovereigns. What would the clergy do? They had all sworn to "be faithful and bear true allegiance to" King James. They had all taught that it was sin to resist the Lord's Anointed. Crabb at Monksland had no scruples about being a Complier. He argued that James had broken his oaths, and so all his subjects were absolved from theirs. But Webb at Durford was in a different position. He honestly believed that Divine Right, Non-resistance, and Passive Obedience were "not only the distinguishing characteristics of this Church, but Principal Points of Christianity." He felt that his oath to James was binding as long as that king lived. He was willing to recognize William as Regent, but could not acknowledge him as King. He refused to take the new oath, and eight Bishops, including the Archbishop and saintly Bishop Ken, and about four hundred beneficed clergy, did the same. Six months later (Feb., 1690) he was evicted from the Vicarage, and found shelter in the Manor House, which Horace de Quetivel, true to the old family tradition of loyalty to lost causes, now made a harbour of refuge for Jacobites and Non-Jurors, while Humphrey Beale, a Whig and a Latitude man, came to be Vicar of Durford.

The Non-Jurors had now to face the question, Could

they remain in communion with the Church as private persons. Their answer was No. The Communion Service, the Litany, Morning and Evening Prayer, all alike were tainted with sinful prayers for the Dutch usurper. Archbishop Sancroft declared that those who attended their parish churches "would need Absolution at the end as well as the beginning of the Service". Moreover all who recognized in any way the intruded Bishops were guilty of the sin of schism, and therefore excommunicate. "Those Priests or Bishops, who dare Usurp the Thrones of Rightful Canonical Bishops invalidly, unjustly and illegally deprived, are very Corahs from whom the Lord's People ought to separate. They can perform no valid Acts of Priesthood. Their very Prayers are Sin. Their Sacraments are no Sacraments. They and all that adhere to them are out of the Church; they can claim no Benefits of God's promises, no not of His Assisting Grace, nor of the Remission of Sins through the Merits of Christ's Blood." Believing this, the only course open to the Non-Jurors was to organize themselves into a separate Church, which they did, declaring that theirs was the only true Church of England, ordaining fresh clergy and consecrating fresh bishops to continue the succession, which did not die out till 1805. But long before then they had disappeared from our village.

A Latitudinarian

Humphrey Beale, the new vicar (1690), was a typical Latitude man. Puritans and Non-Jurors were both alike to him crack-brained fanatics. On all points of doctrine he was bored and indifferent. It was hopeless, he held, to try to understand all Divine truth. The really essential parts of Christianity are quite clear and simple. Why could not foolish people be content with those? Anything more always led men to be nonsensical and immoderate. His sermons were largely made up of phrases culled from those of Tillotson, the new Archbishop of Canterbury: "Christianity is the most reasonable religion in the world". "It requires of us only such things as do approve themselves to the best reason of mankind." "We must take care not to go out of our depths, and lose ourselves in profound inquiry into the deep things of God." "Zeal is dangerous, even in the hands of wise men, and to be governed and kept in with a strict rein; otherwise it will transport them to the doing of undue and irregular things." "The best way to preserve a right judgement in matters of religion is to take great care of good life." "If we be careful to do our best, we shall be accepted of God." A dry, cold, sterile creed, a religion from which all the poetry and all the fire, the colour and all the beauty, all the romance and all the mystery, had been carefully eliminated, a religion which made the eighteenth century, which we are just entering, the dullest and least fruitful period of our Church's history.

Under Queen Anne

These were the days when the squire was king of the village, and the vicar had to take a very subordinate place. Sir Roger de Quetivel, when his father died, returned to the Established Church, and, if we wish to picture him, we can hardly do better than look at the delightful sketch which Addison drew of his friend Sir Roger de Coverley: "Sir Roger, being a good Churchman, has beautified the Inside of his Church with several Texts of his own chusing. He has often told me that at his coming to his Estate he found his Parishioners very irregular; and that, in order to make them kneel and join in the Responses, he gave everyone of them a Hassock and a Common Prayer Book, and at the same time employed an itinerant Singing Master to instruct them rightly in the tunes of the Psalms. As Sir Roger is Landlord to the whole Congregation, he keeps them in very good Order, and will suffer no Body to sleep besides himself; for, if by chance he has been surprized into a short Nap at Sermon, upon recovering out of it, he stands up, and, if he sees any Body else nodding, either wakes them himself, or sends his Servants to them. Sometimes he stands up, when every Body else is upon their Knees, to count the Congregation, or see if any of his Tenants are missing. As soon as the Sermon is finished, no Body presumes to stir, till Sir Roger is gone out of the Church. The Knight walks down from his Seat in the Chancel, between a double Row of his Tenants, that stand bowing to him on each Side, and every now and then enquires how such a one's Wife or Mother or Son or Father do, whom he does not see at Church, which is understood as a secret Reprimand to the Person that is absent."

When Beale died, Sir Roger "desired a Friend of his at the University to find him out a clergyman, rather of plain Sense than of much Learning, of a good Aspect, a clear Voice, a sociable Temper, and, if possible, a Man that understood a little of Back Gammon." "At his first settling with me," he said, "I made him a Present of all the good Sermons, which have been preached in English, and only begged of him, that every Sunday he would pronounce one of them from the Pulpit." So long as the old Squire lived, everything in the village was very decorous and orderly. The people came to church on Sunday. Some of them were really devout in a quiet, humdrum sort of way. Duty was the most emphatic word in their conception of religion; the Christian must do his duty to God and his duty to his neighbour.

A Deist

But old Sir Roger was succeeded by his nephew Terence, a gorgeous person in frills and muff and ruffles and a perfumed wig, which fell in ringlets half-way down his back; from his gold-laced hat to his gold-buckled shoes an Exquisite of the finest water. He was a friend and flatterer of Frederick, Prince of Wales, and a member of the new Dilettante Club, the qualifications for which were habitual drunkenness and a visit to Italy. Yet even he had inherited something of the family interest in Theology, and liked to pose as a champion of the shallow and confident Deism, which was fast becoming the creed of polite society. The old Squire's favourite Sunday books, "The Whole Duty of Man," Nelson's "Companion to the Fasts and Festivals," and Synge's "Gentleman's Religion," were banished to the top shelf, and their place taken by intruders with a very different message. Here was Toland's "Christianity not Mysterious" (1697) with its bold assertion that a true Christianity can contain nothing but plain, demonstrable truths, and that, since the historic creed of Christendom was full of "unreasonable" mysteries, it clearly could not be true Christianity at all. Here was poor crazy Woolston's "Discourses on the Miracles" (1729), calling our Lord "a strolling fortune-teller," and explaining the story of Cana by the fact that the guests had "well drunk". Here was Tindal's "Christianity as old as the Creation" (1730), contrasting the God of Nature with the God of Christian Theology very much to the disadvantage of the latter. "I believe in a Great Supreme Being enormously remote from this world" – this was the fashionable creed in early Hanoverian England – "I believe in a Religion of Nature, as old as the Creation, so perfect as to leave no need of room for any later revelation, either Jewish or Christian. I believe that most of the Bible is a tissue of fables and folly. I believe that the Pagan doctrine of the immortality of the soul is a plausible hypothesis, but the Christian doctrine of the resurrection of the body is utterly opposed to reason. I believe in the forgiveness of sins, for the Distant Deity is so indulgent and sin such a trivial thing, that pardon must follow as a matter of course."

Absentee Vicars

When the man who knew a little of backgammon died, the new Squire gave the living to Simon Parre, a wag who had tickled his sense of humour with some stories out of Rabelais in a London coffee-house. But as Parre already had six livings in various parts of the country, he never troubled Durford with his presence. He accepted the £50 a year as a slight addition to his income, and contracted with a Canterbury curate to do the absolutely necessary work for £15 a year. The blight of pluralities and non-residence had now settled down in England. For a quarter of a century the village never saw its vicar, except on one occasion, when a pompous and irritable stranger in a full-bottomed wig arrived to settle some dispute about the letting of the glebe. Parre was succeeded by Robert Holt, keeper of the Archives at Oxford, who laboriously collected in the next few years a vast amount of detailed information about village life in Attica in the time of Pericles, but never knew to the end of his days whether Durford was in Kent or Cumberland. He in his turn was succeeded by a gentleman named Supple, who spent most of his time conducting young noblemen on continental tours. But he had not altogether forgotten that he was by profession a divine. Had he not published two fat little octavo volumes – "A Defence of Moderation in the Practice of Religion," and a "Vindication of the Divine Ordinance of Tithes"? Meanwhile on Sundays, if the weather was not too unpleasant, a curate rode out from Canterbury to conduct a service. The time of his arrival was quite uncertain, for he did duty in four parishes before he reached Durford, and weddings, funerals, baptisms, were always liable to delay him, since every kind of service had to wait for his weekly visit. Dibble the clerk used to climb the tower to watch for the coming of the parson, and ring the bell, when he saw him begin to cross the marshes. The curate would gallop up to the door, fling a grimy surplice loosely over his shoulders, rattle through the morning service to half a dozen people who had hurriedly assembled, take a baptism and a funeral, toss off a glass of ale, and disappear over the brow of the hill on his way to the next village.

The Church in Ruins

Under such a system the church grew every year more shabby and neglected. The village boys broke the windows, and no one troubled to repair them. A mouldy smell from the De Quetivel vaults came up through the broken floor. The rain and snow poured in through a dozen holes in the roof. The damp traced fantastic patterns of green upon the walls. Strange kinds of fungus flourished in the corners of the pews. The only bit of fresh paint in the whole building was the huge board with the list of benefactors on the west wall, which the Bishops were everywhere insisting on at this time, because so many benefactions had disappeared. The mildewed, rat-eaten Registers were piled on the floor just behind the font. Outside, the churchyard was a wilderness of docks and nettles, concealing fallen tombstones, and even skulls and bones. Well might Addison declare that there was "less appearance of religion in England than in any neighbouring kingdom". For the first time for twelve centuries Durford Church had ceased to have any appreciable influence on the village life.

Chapter 13
How the Church awoke from slumber

John Wesley

At Monksland the state of things was just as bad, till one day there came riding up the hill a trim little figure in cassock, knee-breeches, and black silk stockings, the old correct clerical dress which was fast going out of fashion, with reins lying loose on his horse's neck, and hands grasping a small volume held up to his eyes. It was John Wesley, Fellow of Lincoln College, Oxford, who, ever since that day in 1738 when he first grasped the full meaning of St. Paul's great doctrine of Justification, had given himself to the work of a wandering missioner, riding eight thousand miles a year up and down England, preaching the Gospel wherever he could find men and women to listen to him. Outside the Chequers a group of idlers watched the coming of the stranger with a vague interest, which quickened into blank amazement, when he dismounted, climbed on to a low wall, and began to speak. Gradually it dawned upon their dull minds that he was preaching them a sermon; a parson, obviously a scholar and a gentleman, preaching in the open air! The incredible news spread like wildfire through the village, and almost the entire population came running up to listen. Before long they began to realize that this was no ordinary sermon. The stranger's voice was very quiet. He told no anecdotes. He employed no tricks of oratory. But his words had a steel-like edge. His solemn and transparent earnestness was most disquieting. The swift abrupt sentences came with the rush and impact of bullets. As he reasoned in that calm, level voice of his of sin and judgement to come, the most hardened evil-doers trembled; they saw the horror of sin, they saw the reality of God, no longer a dim, remote Figure, but a Saviour close at hand, waiting with outstretched arms to welcome all who would hear and come.

A Methodist Society

As he finished, a score of them drew near, and begged him with tears in their eyes to teach them more of these things. Enoch Grey, the smith, offered his forge, and there behind closed doors Wesley examined them, and prayed with them, and formed them into a little society, and appointed Enoch as their leader. With his own hands he then wrote out a code of rules which they pledged themselves to obey:

"1. Abstain from evil, especially buying and selling on the Sabbath. Neither sell nor buy anything that has not paid the duty. Defraud not the King any more than your fellow-subject. Never think of being religious, unless you are honest.

"2. Taste no spirituous liquor. Pawn nothing, no not to save life. Wear no needless ornaments, such as rings, earrings, necklaces. Use no needless self-indulgence, such as taking snuff or tobacco.

"3. Use private prayer every day, and family prayer, if you are head of a family.

"4. Keep to the Church. They that do this best, prosper most in their souls. I suffer no meetings under any pretext to be held during Church hours. When Methodists leave the Church, God will leave them.

"5. Lose no opportunity of receiving the Sacrament. All who have neglected this have suffered loss. Most of them are as dead as stone.

"6. Meet in class once a week. Whoever misses class thrice together, thereby excludes himself. Meet the brethren or leave them. It is not honest to profess yourself of a Society, and not obey the rules thereof."

For a time the new converts loyally obeyed their instructions. Every Sunday they filled two benches in their parish church, to the amazement of the curate, who had never seen so large a congregation before; and on Sunday night and Wednesday evening they gathered in the forge for informal devotional meetings of their own. But souls new born, aflame with zeal and desire for worship, could find but little satisfaction in the slovenly, formal, lifeless service of the eighteenth century, and the curate did all that he could to make it even less acceptable by reading a set of dreary sermons on the sin of enthusiasm, which an enterprising Canterbury bookseller let out on hire to clergy who were troubled by the presence of Methodists in their parishes. Meanwhile Enoch Grey developed a gift of rugged, homely exposition. The services in the forge grew more and more attractive; those in the church more and more intolerable. In spite of strong remonstrances from Wesley, the Churchmanship of Monksland Methodists grew more and more nominal. In time they began to hold their meetings during Church hours. Later a red brick preaching-house was built, and licensed under the Conventicle Act as a dissenting place of worship. Enoch Grey and all his followers were lost to the Church.

An Early Evangelical

When Wesley left Monksland and rode on to Durford, he found a far happier state of things. The degenerate heir of the house of De Quetivel, after wasting all his substance on quadrille and basset, had offered for sale the advowson of the living of which he was patron. His advertisement happened to catch the eye (1760) of John Thornton of Clapham, Director of the Russia Company, who was using his wealth to provide a more spiritual type of clergy for every parish he could influence. He promptly bought the patronage and appointed Charles Stennett as vicar. Stennett, while curate of a city church, had ridden out to Blackheath to see one of the open-air services which George Whitefield, Wesley's friend and fellow-worker, was conducting. He had gone to scoff, but had remained to pray.

His whole conception of Christianity was transformed by that visit. On the following Sunday he scandalized his decorous city congregation by a fervent sermon on the text "Redemption through His Blood." Monday found him dismissed from his curacy and without the smallest prospect of being able to find another. Fortunately a rumour of his sermon had reached the Countess of Huntingdon, the benevolent lady who was playing the part of a "mother in Israel" to the few scattered and persecuted clergy who had been touched with the spirit of the Revival. For a year or two Stennett acted as one of her chaplains. Now that he was Vicar of Durford, Wesley knew that in that part of Kent there was always one church and vicarage, in which he would never fail to find the warmest welcome.

Thus the Revival had an opposite effect upon the two villages. At Monksland it made the Church even weaker and colder than before, for the real spiritual life of the place now centred round the forge. At Durford it made the Church a new power and source of blessing. It meant a great change to have once more a resident vicar, but no one guessed how great the change would be. Cobbin the clerk was told again and again that he was a liar, when he spread the news that the new vicar meant to have ten services in church every week, besides at least half a dozen other meetings. Every day there was going to be service at five o'clock in the morning that every one might begin his day's work with prayer. On Sundays, besides the morning and afternoon services, the church was going to be lighted with candles for an evening service. Another candlelight service would be held every Thursday evening. Nor was this all. In flat defiance of the Conventicle Act, which forbade any service except in church or a licensed dissenting chapel, Stennett arranged with two old women in outlying hamlets to hold services in their cottages on Monday and Friday. On Sundays there was a Prayer Meeting in the vicarage kitchen at six o'clock in the morning, and another meeting for prayer and hymn-singing at the close of evening service. There was a Prayer Meeting every Tuesday evening, and, as men and women expressed a desire for a better life, Stennett formed them into a little society which met at his house on Wednesdays.

Hymn-singing

At first the village scoffed loudly at these unheard-of methods; but curiosity made them come to see what it all meant, and, when they came, they heard something which made them come again. Hymn-singing too in church was a daring but delightful innovation. Hitherto the only music had been one of Sternhold and Hopkins' Psalms, roared as a solo by Cobbin the clerk. But Stennett had brought down from London with him a box of Martin Madan's collection of "Psalms and Hymns". Hobbs and Dobbs found themselves now invited to sing "Love Divine, all love excelling," and "Jesu, Lover of my soul." Moreover the west gallery was given over to the choir. Mund the Miller was asked to bring his beloved violoncello. Old Master Sage the Ditcher brought his key-bugle. Some one else was discovered to own a hautboy, and some one else a bassoon. Many certainly possessed strong and musical voices, and were proud to be in the church choir. The whole parish began to get interested once more in the services. It quickly grew ashamed of the dirty and dilapidated state of the church building, and set to work strenuously to clean and repair it. And soon a new gallery had to be added to accommodate the congregation.

The Sunday School

In 1784, Stennett read an account of the Sunday School which Robert Raikes had started for the urchins of Gloucester, and he determined that Durford should have a Sunday School also. Old Mother Ayles was very proud of the fact that she could read, and for a shilling a week she was glad to promise to receive in her cottage as many children as the Vicar could persuade to attend, "there to teach them to spell and read the Bible and the Prayer Book for two hours every Sabbath morning and for two hours every Sabbath afternoon, and to bring the children to Church to Morning and Afternoon Service." The Churchwardens' Account Book records the fact that on the following Easter, the "Sacrament Money was applied for the purpose to purchase eleven spelling-books, forty-eight catechism books, four hornbooks, and six Testaments for the Sunday School".

A Simeonite

When at last, after forty years of faithful persevering work, Stennett passed to his rest, John Desmond came from Clapham to be Vicar of Durford. As a boy he had gone to Hull Grammar School, and there, like so many other lads who did grand work for God in later years, he had fallen strongly under the influence of Joseph Milner, the headmaster. The Elland Society, which had been founded (1777) to help promising young Evangelicals who hoped to take orders, had sent him to Cambridge, where he had entered Queens' which his old head-master's brother Isaac was making a training ground for Evangelical clergy. Here he had become an eager disciple of Charles Simeon, Incumbent of Trinity Church, and in his famous Bible Class and Sermon Class and Conversation Circle had learnt how to give convincing reasons for the faith that was in him. Then he had gone to Clapham to be curate to John Venn, and thus had come in close touch with that remarkable group of laymen, whom Sydney Smith maliciously nicknamed the Clapham Sect. To have known Henry Thornton, the banker, and William Wilberforce, the most brilliant speaker in the House of Commons, and Charles Grant, the Chairman of the East India Company, and Lord Teignmouth, who had been Governor-General of India, and Zachary Macaulay, who had been Governor of Sierra Leone, to have worshipped with them, to have watched at close quarters their strenuous and self-denying piety, to have had some share in the stubborn fight that they were waging against the slave trade, was a better education for a young man even than Simeon's Bible Classes.

The Great Societies

He came to Durford full of zeal and determination to guide the deep and fervent piety, which his predecessor had fostered, into channels of self-denial and sacrifice for others. The Church Missionary Society had been founded in 1799, and every year Durford now had its missionary collection. A Penny Association was formed to collect from door to door. Occasionally some great preacher arrived from London in a post-chaise heavily laden with reports and pamphlets, one of the Evangelical leaders, who was giving seven weeks to the work of visiting the villages to stir up enthusiasm for the missionary cause. One society after another was founded in rapid succession, and Durford folk were expected to do what they could for them all. The Bible Society began its work (1804) of supplying every nation in the world with Bibles in its own language. The Jews' Society undertook the task (1809) of trying to win the whole Jewish race at home and abroad. Churchmen, even in obscure villages like Durford, were learning to dream dreams and to think imperially.

The Napoleon Scare

And this is the more remarkable as they had other urgent matters to attend to. Just across the Straits of Dover in the great camp at Boulogne was "the Corsican Ogre" with 160,000 veterans, waiting for a moonless night, when our Admiral's back was turned, to slip across the Channel in his flat-bottomed boats. The west end of the church was blocked with the parish firelocks, and all the able-bodied men in the village spent two hours drilling every Sunday afternoon. Behind the church, on the brow of the hill, stood the great beacon, ready to give the alarm as soon as the French should land. Every man knew his special duty and was never tired of discussing it. Crabstock and his sons were to go to the marshes, and block every sluice, so that they should be flooded. Churchwarden Drain with one party would destroy the roads. Churchwarden Broyd with another party would collect all the horses and cattle, and entrust them to reliable men to drive far inland. Farmer Brant was responsible for seeing that all the corn and provisions were burnt. In the hour of danger the parish church became the natural centre of all the patriotic fervour of the village. Many a special service was held, and in a corner of the church safe still lie a bundle of the prayers "issued by his Majesty's Special Command" for use on these occasions; some very anxious and uneasy – "We are threatened with invasion by a fierce and haughty foe, for that we alone among the Nations are found to withstand his Ambition"; others jubilant and triumphant – "We acknowledge with thankful hearts Thy great goodness in the glorious success which Thou hast vouchsafed unto the fleet of our Sovereign," till at last we reach the form of thanksgiving for Waterloo – "Grant that the result of this mighty battle, terrible in conflict, but glorious beyond example in success, may put an end to the miseries of Europe, and stanch the blood of the nations."

A Low Churchman

Monksland also now possessed a resident vicar. The Bishops were beginning to bring steady pressure on their clergy to live in their parishes, though it took more than another generation before the evils of non-residence were generally overcome. But very few were Evangelicals, like the Vicar of Durford. Most of the clergy belonged to the school of which Lawrence Peke of Monksland was a favourable example. He was the Squire's younger brother. His professional duties were one Sunday service, weddings, funerals, and an occasional visit to the sick, if sent for. When the spread of Methodism stirred him up to start a second service, he entered a cautious note in the Church Register: "I, Lawrence Peke, Vicar, do hereby declare that

I am not bound by any obligation whatever to serve this Church twice on Sunday, but that I am influenced thereto purely upon conscientious motives, and that I think myself at liberty to discontinue it at any time, whenever there appears to me cause or reason for so doing." On weekdays he lived just like his neighbours, distinguished only by his white neck cloth and a greater watchfulness in his own words and actions. He farmed his own glebe, and he farmed it well. No one in the parish knew more than he about hops, or oilcake, or turnips. He was a keen sportsman, and shot and hunted regularly. Once a year he always rode into Canterbury for the races. As a magistrate he was a terror to evil-doers. Every one in the parish called him "the master," the person who was responsible for keeping order, and who knew how to keep it. About theology he knew nothing, and he cared less. His message was summed up in the single clause misquoted from the Catechism, "Do your duty in the state of life into which it has pleased God to call you". He disliked Dissenters, but he abominated Evangelicals, and he sent his son to Oxford to escape the influence of Simeon.

A Parish Clerk

Another person of almost equal importance in the village was Jerry Briscall, parish clerk, and landlord of the Chequers. No one then saw anything strange in this combination of duties, nor in the response which he always added to the end of each funeral service, "Friends of the corpse is respectfully requested to call at my house for refreshments." On Sunday he was an imposing figure in wig and horn spectacles, thundering out "Arummen" at the close of every prayer, from the lowest compartment of the great three decker, which formed clerk's desk, reading desk, and pulpit. He regarded the service as a duologue between himself and the Vicar, and on one occasion when a rash stranger ventured to join in the responses he looked up with the fierce query, "Who's that interrupting?" It was his privilege to choose and announce the Psalm from Sternhold and Hopkins – for, of course, nothing so Methodistical as a hymn was tolerated – "Let us sing to the praise and glory of God the hundred and twelfth Psalm," an invitation which no one ever dreamed of accepting, except the choir of three men and a boy in the west gallery, who practised every Saturday night under his supervision in the bar-parlour.

A Liberal

Meanwhile for forty years Desmond remained Vicar of Durford, for these were the days when Evangelical clergy hardly ever changed their parishes, but in his old age two new movements arose, which disquieted and distressed him. Young Thomas de Quetivel went to Rugby and then to Oriel, and returned eager to discuss with his old god-father the new ideas that he had learnt from Arnold and the Liberals. He brought home Milman's "History of the Jews" (1830), the first attempt by any English clergyman to treat the Old Testament story from a "strictly historical, not theological" standpoint. Here Desmond to his horror found the chosen people of God described as though they had been an ordinary Oriental tribe; Abraham was a "Sheikh," Joseph a "Vizier," the Judges were "guerilla leaders"; and with great ingenuity a natural explanation was suggested for every miracle. Equally startling from another point of view was Arnold's "Principles of Church Reform" (1833), which pleaded passionately that Churchmen, Presbyterians, Congregationalists, Baptists, and Methodists should combine to form one Church, "thoroughly national, thoroughly united, thoroughly Christian, which should allow great varieties of opinion and of ceremonies and of forms of worship according to the various knowledge and habits and tempers of its members, while it truly held one common faith, and trusted in one common Saviour, and worshipped one common God". Episcopacy must be retained, but an Episcopacy "divested of all those points against which the objections of Dissenters have been particularly levelled." "Episcopalians will be satisfied, if the mere name of Bishop is preserved." The Prayer Book should be used once a Sunday, but any number of "freer and more social services" might be "performed at different times of the day within the walls of the same church."

A Tractarian

But, if old-fashioned Evangelicals were alarmed by what the Liberals proposed, one little group of another school was stung into vehement opposition. Keble, the gentle Vicar of Hursley, startled Oxford (1833) by a sermon on National Apostasy. Newman, to whom an ever-increasing number of undergraduates gave an almost adoring hero-worship, declared that Liberalism was Antichrist. And young Walter Peke of Monksland had become one of his most fervent pupils and disciples. He had not missed one of Newman's famous sermons in St. Mary's or of his lectures in Adam de Brome's dark and dreary little chapel. And now he was enrolled as a "Propagandist" of the new Association of Friends of the Church. Authority, Discipline, Mystery – these were the three master words around which his thoughts turned. And one day (1833) he rode into Durford with saddle-bags bursting with a series of "Tracts for the Times," of which Newman was editor and the moving spirit. "Magnify your office," was the cry of these Tracts to the clergy. "Make men familiar with the thought of the Church, living, catholic, continuous. Lift high its authority against that of rebellious reason and the apostate state. Without valid Sacraments no soul can be sure of salvation; and valid Sacraments can nowhere be found, save in a Church which can show Apostolic Succession. It is impossible to exaggerate the unique position of the Church of which you are ministers, the very Church which Christ founded, the Church which still possesses all the powers and prerogatives that He gave it, the appointed channel of grace for God's people, the pillar and the ground of truth." Desmond read the Tracts carefully, but they left him unconvinced. To him life was far more important than organization; the value of a Church depended on the spiritual life of its members. "It is not by exalting its ancient pedigree that our Church will be saved," he said, "but by filling its ranks with truly converted Christians."

The Romeward Drift

He and Peke had many an opportunity of discussing these points together, for the latter came to the family living of Monksland, but the more Desmond saw of the Oxford movement, the less he liked it. It began with an honest desire to magnify the position of the Church of England, but it soon became clear that not a few of the younger men were drifting into an attitude of scorn for the Church of their baptism, and of wistful admiration for the Church of Rome. "I hate the Reformation and the Reformers," wrote Froude. "I utterly reject and anathematize," wrote Parker, "the principle of Protestantism." "We are little satisfied with our position," wrote Dalgairns to a French newspaper, "we groan at the sins committed by our ancestors in separating from the Catholic world. We love with unfeigned affection the Apostolic See, which we acknowledge to be the head of Christendom." "Were we to pursue," wrote Ward in his "Ideal of a Christian Church," "such a line of conduct as has here been sketched, we should be taught from above to discern the plain marks of Divine wisdom and authority in the Roman Church, to repent in sorrow and bitterness of heart over our great sin in deserting her communion, and to sue humbly at her feet for pardon and restoration."

Tract XC

But nothing gave so great a shock to Churchmen of every other school as the ninetieth Tract (1841) which was Newman's answer to the question, "What do you make of the Thirty-Nine Articles? Surely they commit the Church to a definitely anti-Roman position!" His answer was to plead three points which he thought indisputable: (1) that the modern creed of Rome is contained in the decrees of the Council of Trent, and the decrees which dealt with such points as Purgatory, Pardon, Relics, and the Sacrifice of the Mass had not been issued at the time when our Articles were drawn up: therefore the Articles were not directed against the official creed of Rome, as we know it;[1] (2) that in the days before the Council of Trent popular Romish belief and practice had far outrun the authorized dogmatic standards of the Church; and (3) that at the time the Articles were published hope had not been abandoned of including all who still sympathized with the old ways within the Church of England. From this he drew the conclusion that, when the Articles declare "the Romish doctrine concerning purgatory" to be "a fond thing vainly invented," or transubstantiation to be "repugnant to the plain words of Scripture," or "the sacrifice of masses" to be "blasphemous fables and dangerous deceits," they are only attacking some unauthorized superstitions and corruptions, which cautious Roman theologians would themselves have condemned. "The Protestant Confession was drawn up with the purpose of including Catholics; and Catholics will not now be excluded." Newman was undoubtedly perfectly sincere. "I was utterly without any idea," he wrote, "that my Tract would make any disturbance." But to many of his readers the Tract appeared a most insidious and uncandid piece of special pleading, an attempt

---

[1] The historical question was more complicated than Newman seemed to realize. The Council of Trent lasted from 1545 to 1563. The Articles were begun in 1549, issued 1553 and revised 1562. The decrees of 16 out of the 25 sessions of the Council were known in England before the first issue of the Articles; the decrees of 22 before the revision of 1562. And though Newman was right in saying that Articles 22 and 31 were issued before the decrees of Trent on these points were drafted, the English divines had plenty of evidence before them to show what those decrees would almost certainly be.

to explain away perfectly straightforward language; and a storm of protest arose. The Hebdomadal Council of his University censured it; bishop after bishop condemned it; and Newman bowed before the tempest. The Tracts were discontinued. Their editor withdrew to his country parish of Littlemore. Then came the news that one by one the Oxford men were being received into the Church of Rome. Ward and Dalgairns went over in September (1845), Newman himself and Oakeley and Bowles and Stanton in October, Faber in November, Coffin, Vicar of St. Mary Magdalene, Oxford, in December. Men said for the moment that the Oxford Movement was dead. But they were mistaken. Pusey remained, and Keble.

A Ritualist

This year gave each of the villages a new vicar. To Monksland came Cyril Loaming, a young Oxford man, full of enthusiasm for vessels and vestments and mediaeval ritual. The recent controversy had called attention to the Church of Rome. High Churchmen had attended Roman services and studied Roman service-books. And even those who felt no desire to leave the Church of their baptism, began to wish to bring back into their Church many of the rites and ceremonies which had been banished or dropped at the time of the Reformation. For some years Loaming's experiments were rather amateurish, but in 1857 Purchas' "Directorium Anglicanum" led to a great advance in the ritual movement. It was written to "put the Priest of the nineteenth century on a par with the Priest of the sixteenth as to ritual knowledge". "Ritual and ceremonial are the hieroglyphics of the Catholic religion, a language understanded of the faithful, a kind of parable in action." "As there is but one Catholic Church, so the ritual of every portion thereof will have a family likeness." "Hence this attempt to read our rubrics by the light of the pre-reformation service-books." Loaming learnt that he must banish his oak Communion Table, and erect an altar with a slab "either of stone or marble". On it must stand a cross and two altar lights "of pure white wax," except on certain occasions when they are to be "coloured with gamboge". He must add to his Church wardrobe an alb, an amice and a cotta, and sets of chasubles, copes, maniples, tunics and dalmatics, varying in colour with the Church seasons. For the Holy Communion he must use only wafer bread; common baker's bread is "unseemly and irreverent". He may vary the colour of the wine, "white on ferial days, red on festivals". He learnt what Latin prayers from the Sarum Missal he should secretly interpolate into the Prayer-Book Office, and what attitude he and his servers should take at every point in the service. He learnt, too, how to make the singing of the Magnificat a solemn and elaborate rite, during which he and little Dan, the ploughman's youngest son, did mysterious things with a censer amid clouds of incense. He learnt how to exorcise salt, and make with it Holy Water that "whatever is touched or sprinkled by it may be freed from all uncleanness". Services in Monksland church began to bear some dim and faint resemblance to the services that had been held there before the monks were driven from the Abbey, but with this great difference. In those days the little church was filled with villagers on Sunday. Now the majority went nowhere. Some went to the Methodist chapel. Only a few were laboriously learning to find in the Catholic ritual some real expression of their own religious experience.

The Higher Criticism

Meanwhile Durford, too, had received a new vicar. John Fortescue was appointed as an Evangelical, but he soon began to call himself a Broad Churchman. In the middle of the nineteenth century many religious men passed through a period of grave doubt and perplexity, as they struggled to adjust their old creed to the new truths revealed by science and the growth of secular knowledge. The great majority of English clergy had been brought up to believe that "every word, every syllable, every letter of the Bible is just what it would be had God spoken from heaven without any human intervention. Every scientific statement is infallibly accurate"[1]. "The Bible is none other than the Voice of Him that sitteth on the throne. Every book of it, every chapter of it, every verse of it, every word of it, every syllable of it, every letter of it, is the direct utterance of the Most High."[2] But this belief was now being roughly assailed from many quarters. In foreign universities Oriental scholars had been ruthlessly at work, testing the date of the various books of the Old Testament by the same critical methods which others were applying to the "Rig Veda" or the Homeric poems. And they had arrived at some very startling conclusions. They declared that the old dates were almost grotesquely false: that the Books of Moses, the Psalms of David, and the Proverbs of Solomon, for example, were written centuries after the death of the heroes whose names they bear; that the greater part of the Old Testament, at all events in its present form, is the work of Jews who lived after the return from Babylon; that only a few of the prophets are earlier, and even their books contain many later interpolations.[3] Daring and reckless pioneers now began to introduce these new ideas into England, and the most headstrong and impetuous of all was Bishop Colenso, who, in "The Pentateuch Examined" (1862), challenged not only the dates of the books, but their historical value. Moses was "a personage quite as shadowy and unhistorical as our own King Arthur". Joshua "appears to be entirely a mythical character". "The whole of the narrative of Ezra and much of Nehemiah are

---

[1] Baylie's "Verbal Inspiration".
[2] Dean Burgon's "Inspiration and Interpretation", 1861.
[3] It is not the place of this book to discuss the complicated question as to how far later discussions and discoveries have confirmed or shaken the conclusions of these early critics. History simply has to record that at this period a great controversy about these matters suddenly arose.

pure inventions of the chronicler." "There is no infallible Book for our guidance, as there is no infallible Church."

Natural Science

Meanwhile geology and botany and biology and many a kindred science were beginning to make confident statements, which were very bewildering to believers in the Bible. Ever since Sir Charles Lyall published his "Principles of Geology" (1830), his followers had grown more and more dogmatic in their assertions, that the world could not have been created in seven days. They pointed to the white cliffs of Dover, built up of minute shells of marine organisms at the rate of an inch or two a century; they pointed to the buried forests in our coal fields, and protested that these were facts, which it was impossible to square with the first chapter of Genesis. And then came Charles Darwin (1859) with his startling theory that, so far from man being created on the sixth day, he too had been slowly evolved through incalculable ages from an ape, a fish, a tiny cell in some putrescent fungus. Theologians like Bishop Wilberforce rushed into the fray, and were badly beaten on the unfamiliar ground, and theology and religion had to suffer the discredit of their defeat. And many a puzzled country parson, such as John Fortescue, turned from theology in despair, and threw himself heart and soul into plain, practical problems, better cottages for the labourers, night schools, lending libraries and allotments, working men's clubs, poor law reform, penny banks, and health lectures, all good and useful things, which made him immensely popular, but poor substitutes for that Bread of Life without which no soul can live.

The Twentieth Century

But this crisis passed away, as many another had done. When John English became Vicar of Durford the early panic was over. He had faced his doubts and found answers to them before his ordination. He handled his

Bible in a way rather different from that of some older men; he did not expect to find in a volume written centuries ago all the latest formulae of modern physical science; but it was to him still the Word of God, the supreme authority on all questions of religion. Even though critics should succeed in proving that Jewish Rabbis had fixed wrong dates to many of the sacred books, even though we may be as ignorant of the author of Genesis as we are of the author of Judges, the books themselves still remain in all their majesty and beauty, a medium through which God's people will ever hear His Voice. If evolutionists should be able to demonstrate that the process by which God "formed man of the dust of the ground" was one which lasted more than a million years, they still will have to remember, that it is one thing to trace the stages in a process, another to explain the cause. The majestic words remain true "In the beginning God created the Heaven and the Earth." And English was able, with faith unshaken, to take up his work of seeking to win for God the men who follow the plough. From the Evangelical Movement he had inherited a sense of the importance of each individual soul, of the worthlessness of any Churchmanship that is not based on personal religion; from the Oxford Movement he had inherited a sense of value of the Church, of the duty of each individual to take his appointed place within the great Brotherhood founded by Christ Himself; from the Broad Church Movement he had inherited a desire to face facts fearlessly and frankly; and his work was not in vain. There are some in his parish who hate the good and love the evil; there are some whose profession to serve God is only an empty sham; but so there have been in every age of our village history. The Great War roused the Church to make its constitution democratic. Parliament was persuaded to give churchmen for the first time since the Reformation liberty to manage their own affairs. A chain of councils was created, a Parochial Church Council for every parish, elected by all members of the Church over eighteen years old, a Ruridecanal Conference for every rural deanery, a Diocesan Conference for every diocese, and a National Church Assembly for the whole of England. No longer would the great things of the Church be settled by a secular Parliament containing many non-Churchmen. No longer would the little things be settled round the family tea-table by the Vicar and his daughters. All matters, both great and small, must now be discussed by the elected Councils. Durford voted for its first Parochial Church Council in 1921. So Hodge the ploughman, ex-sergeant in the Royal Fusiliers, took his seat side by side with Sir Cyril de Quetivel, the Squire.

CHAPTER 14
How the Church enlarged its vision

THE years between 1918 and 1939 saw rapid changes throughout the world and throughout Britain, changes from which Durford and Monksland could not escape. Both were sufficiently near to London to feel the weight of the new building programme; Monksland became a residential area, commuters doubling the population with their well built houses and landscaped gardens in that part of the parish around the manor. But the Squire found few of them accompanying him to church on Sundays. Instead, they would fill up their cars and spend the day at the seaside in summer, while bridge parties and the early radio programmes kept them amused at home in winter evenings. The new vicar, an ex-Army padre, Godfrey Sharpe, found it hard going to keep a Sunday school alive, to raise his quota for diocesan and central Church funds, and to educate his children. But his wife still ran the large rectory with a cook and housemaid, and a pensioner managed to make the most of a half-acre kitchen garden. Before long, the clergy found it pleasant not to stay for more than five years in their livings, so Monksland had three incumbents in the fifteen years prior to 1939. Each regularly attended the deanery clergy Chapter meetings, but though of varying ages and gifts, none found much encouragement from increased congregations, however strictly they taught the Catholic faith, and prepared their children for Confirmation. Too many candidates lapsed shortly after their first Communion, or attended only at the great festivals.

Recall to Religion

The abdication crisis and the Archbishop's "Recall to

Religion" coincided with the rise to power of Hitler and Mussolini in Europe. Though Derek Potter at Monksland might preach powerfully on the law of morality, and stress the necessity of full membership of the Church to which all should belong, only the new squire, Sir Ernest, and the faithful few were present to heed his exhortations. Church council meetings were increasingly concerned with raising funds to repair the roof over the north aisle, or to buy new carpets for the chancel and sanctuary. Then came "Munich", and many in Monksland rejoiced at the picture of Neville Chamberlain with his umbrella, fresh from his visit to Hitler, waving a white paper, and calling: "Peace in our time"! But others shook their heads; appeasement could only postpone, not prevent war. So came September, 1939, and the German invasion of Poland, with the harsh voice of the Prime Minister announcing two days later that England was at war.

Meanwhile, events at Durford had taken a different course. A gradual increase of population in the 1920's had been followed in the early 1930's by the building of vast new housing estates. Instead of a modest two thousand, the vicar, Eric Goodman, found himself in charge of a parish of more than fifteen thousand, as field after field was covered with houses, and new street patterns appeared. He acquired a curate, and with the full support of his church council, he launched into a parish mission shortly after the coronation of 1937. A large marquee was obtained for a series of children's services; every house was visited, and the special Sunday services were followed by weeknight meetings. By these means, a number of new families were contacted, some of whom became regular worshippers, and a small group of really committed Christians emerged who met weekly for prayer and Bible study. Even with this success, however, Goodman felt that they had hardly touched more than the surface of the population, and the total response was a great disappointment to him and his helpers. His staff meetings included long discussions as to whether new evangelistic methods should be used, but firm agreement was seldom reached as to what these should be. To both parishes, the war brought extensive upheaval. The young men soon found themselves in uniform, and most of the girls not long after, though some remained in the area as members of the Women's Land Army. Thanksgiving for the deliverance of Dunkirk brought full churches at both Monksland and Durford, and earnest prayers were offered for eventual victory. Within weeks, the Battle of Britain was being fought out overhead. The Squire's son, Geoffrey, a fighter pilot, did a victory roll over the manor on his way back to Manston airfield, while his father commanded the Home Guard. Frequent alerts and "all clears" on the sirens disturbed each night. Men kept watch in the church belfries for enemy forces, ready to ring the bells in the event of the expected invasion. Gradually the danger passed, and men's interest turned to Wavell's victories in north Africa, and to the German attack on Russia. Giles Benson, churchwarden of Monksland, now a major in the artillery, sent back as much news as escaped the censor's blue pencil, and his wife Margaret, at home with their two young children, kept their friends informed. Casualties began to come in; one Sunday morning Goodman read out the name of Lieutenant Fred Wilkinson, R.N.V.R., killed in a destroyer action off Crete, and his bereaved parents, who kept a greengrocer's shop in Durford, were remembered in prayer. National Days of Prayer were held, and well observed at both churches. At length the tide began to turn. Though the Japanese air force crippled the American fleet at Pearl Harbour in December, 1941, America came into the war. Churchill's speeches and Montgomery's victory at Alamein brought new heart into the country. At last there was talk of a "second front", and invasion forces for the continent, with all their massive equipment and stores, began to pass through Durford and Monksland on their way to the coast. So came June, 1944, and the "D-day" of invasion took a massive armada across the Channel. There followed disappointment at Arnhem, and Rommel's counter-offensive in the Ardennes, but the end was in sight. At last came victory in Europe in May, 1945, with celebrations throughout the country, followed only a few months later by the dropping of the first atomic bombs, and the surrender of Japan. Roosevelt's "unconditional surrender" had been achieved. But Potter and Goodman were wrestling with many questions: was it morally right for the allies to drop the atom bomb, so condemning many thousands of innocent civilians to slow death? Men knew what they had been fighting against, but what were they really fighting for? What did such words as liberty, and patriotism mean in the mid-twentieth century? Who were the truly free? Had the Church thought out what would happen after the war?

Towards the Conversion of England

In this, the Church had not been idle, and one report appeared in 1945, commissioned by the Church Assembly, of more than usual interest. Entitled "Towards the Conversion of England", it quickly became a best seller. It set out (in its terms of reference) "to survey the whole problem of modern evangelism with special reference to the spiritual needs of the non-worshipping community", and to find out how these needs might be met most effectively. After defining evangelism as "so to present Christ Jesus in the power of the Holy Spirit that men shall come to put their trust in God through Him, to accept Him as their Saviour and serve Him as their King in the fellowship of His Church", it fastened on the contemporary scene. There was a drift from religion, a decline in churchgoing, and a collapse in Christian moral standards. This could be accounted for on many grounds, the report went on; there was the effect of increasing urbanisation, secular education, and the rise of scientific Humanism. Against this background, the report set out a modern re-statement of the Gospel, eternal in its content, but changing in its presentation. It stressed the need to visualize the apostolate of the whole Church; the spiritual work of the parish must not be simply the responsibility of the vicar; indeed, in Archbishop William Temple's words, his main duty must be "to train the lay members of the congregation in their work of witness". For this the clergy themselves needed training, and the setting up of "schools of evangelism" was suggested. Other recommendations included the encouragement of united evangelistic campaigns, much wider use of advertising and literature, and renewed emphasis on adult religious education. The compiling of a new catechism was suggested, on more comprehensive lines than that of the Prayer Book, and a new examination of the Christian doctrine of baptism advised. All this came as a breath of fresh air to young Robert Todd at Durford, but his neighbour at Monksland, Basil Pearson, was hesitant. In this area, as indeed throughout the whole country, the Anglican Church found herself facing a hardening of "party" attitudes within, in contrast to a greater concern for unity with other churches and denominations. For a new and cumbersome word was coming into general use, "ecumenical". It was first brought to popular notice in the enthronement sermon of Archbishop Temple at Canterbury in 1942; "here is the great ground of hope for the coming days – this world-wide Christian fellowship, this ecumenical movement, as it is often called".

The Ecumenical Movement

It all began with the recognition by missionaries overseas that the divisions in the Church which had sent them abroad (as members of Anglican, Methodist, or Baptist missionary societies) were bringing confusion to native Christians in Asia and Africa. A Methodist chapel had been built in Durford in the mid-1850's, and an even older Congregational meeting house was fairly well supported in Monksland. Their purpose was understood, and, after antagonism between "Church" and "Chapel" in the nineteenth century, and indeed up to the outbreak of World War I, a "live and let live" policy involved each small congregation going its separate ways Sunday by Sunday. But at the highest level, a conference of representatives of the world's missionary societies met at Edinburgh in 1910, hesitantly sponsored by Archbishop Davidson of Canterbury. This disclosed the passionate desire of the younger Churches for greater freedom in leadership (there was no Indian bishop till V. S. Azariah was consecrated Bishop of Dornakal in 1912). From this conference, two continuation committees, called Faith and Order, and Life and Work, held periodic meetings in several strategic centres at intervals between the wars. News of this work reached down to, and was considered by diocesan and deanery conferences. After the war, the immediate outstanding development was the formation of the Church of South India in 1947, when four Anglican dioceses united with Methodists, Congregationalists and Presbyterians in that area. Nearly half a million Anglicans lost their separate existence in order to find a new loyalty to a larger united Christian body. This caused some grief in England, and recognition of the new Church was slow. A year later, the World Council of Churches was formed, with an inaugural gathering at Amsterdam. If all these happenings appeared to be far removed from Kentish parishes, yet Durford had the honour of a visit from an African bishop attending the Lambeth Conference of all Anglican bishops in 1948. The deanery was represented there in strength, and members were deeply impressed by the bishop's humility and spiritual power.

The war had brought great changes to that neighbourhood. History was made when the young squire, now Sir Geoffrey, decided that rising costs and shortage of labour would force him to abandon the manor, so breaking a family association of nearly nine hundred years. With great reluctance he sold the house, now too large for him and his wife; it was bought by developers, who proceeded to demolish it, and to build some twenty residential properties, "highly desirable" to professional commuters, which quickly sold at a handsome profit to the builders. Among these were two families who wholeheartedly threw in their lot with the church, providing most welcome support to the parochial church council. Bob Ralston, an architect, and George Bevan, a schoolmaster, quickly made their presence felt, and Robert Todd found himself increasingly making use of their willing help in a number of ways. Both supported with enthusiasm Todd's suggestion that a coachload from the parish should go to Harringay to hear Dr. Billy Graham speak at his campaign in 1954. Several people stayed behind after the meeting for counselling, and over the following weeks and months they were gradually brought into the deeper fellowship of the parish.

The Social Gospel

The 1960's were on the whole a depressing period for the Church. The publication of *Honest to God*, in which a bishop raised many doubts on accepted Christian doctrines, brought relief and intellectual freedom to some, but undermined the faith of others. There was a general failure of nerve on the part of the clergy, a hesitation to preach positively on the old basic doctrines, which were replaced by emphasising the social gospel, stressing the need to help the plight of the hungry and homeless, and the Church's duty to turn words of comfort into action. The popularity of the Beatles and the growth of "pop" culture, blazed forth from transistor radios, indicated a new group consciousness among the young. The more serious-minded took part in marches to Aldermaston, protesting against the manufacture and use of atomic weapons associated with that research centre. Perhaps the most steadying influence on the life of the Church at this time was that exercised by Archbishop Ramsey, who, while recognizing the arguments of the more radical theologians, yet refused to be carried away by their enthusiasm. By his scholarly writings, preaching and lectures, he offered a stabilizing element to which the more thoughtful turned in gratitude.

Moves towards Anglican and Methodist Unity

Moves towards Christian unity were continuing, and a carefully thought out scheme was produced for uniting Anglicans and Methodists. This was most thoroughly debated in the Church Assembly and by the Methodist Conference, while all subsidiary conferences on both sides had ample opportunities to consider the issues involved. These included a proposed inaugural service, at which there should be a mutual laying-on of hands by representative members of both Churches. The move was enthusiastically welcomed by Robert Todd, who had already established good relations with local Methodist ministers, inviting them to preach occasionally in his parish church, especially during the week of prayer for Christian unity each January. Basil Pearson, however, was more hesitant. In what sense did Methodist ministers regard sacramental worship? Would their celebrations of the Eucharist in a united ministry have the same intention as that of the Anglican priesthood? Would those ordained by the new ordination service receive the same gifts as those bestowed by the old? Would acceptance of the scheme divide the Church still further, and what would happen to those who dissented on both sides? While Robert Todd and many like him believed that the answers to these and many other questions could only be discovered by going forward in faith under the guidance of the Holy Spirit, Basil Pearson felt that the whole scheme was too ambiguous, and his more cautious parishioners agreed with him. He was also uneasy about many practical questions which did not appear to have been sufficiently considered. What would happen to the various properties involved? Would Anglican churches always remain standing, and Methodist churches be pulled down and the sites sold? And what of those who preferred the more formal mode of Anglican worship? Would Methodists agree to participate in traditional Anglican rites, or wish to continue with those forms to which they had always been accustomed? Or would both Churches devise new services? In the event, the whole matter was settled by the decision that approval for the scheme must be indicated by a 75% majority in the General Synod. When the vote was taken on 3rd May, 1972, while the Methodists gave the required support, the scheme was passed by the Synod, but without the required overall majority, despite overwhelming episcopal approval. The matter has therefore dropped at the highest level officially, but friendships and joint worship at the grass roots have continued to flourish in all parts of the country.

Synodical Government

Mention of the General Synod indicates the step forward taken by the Church of England in introducing full synodical government. This brought to an end the old Church Assembly after fifty years of service, and the establishment of a new and smaller body, of which the House of Laity is a full member. The position of Convocation is now somewhat ambiguous. It is elected for a period of five years, and is not automatically dissolved at each General Election. It now meets as a separate body only when called upon to do so in order to discuss some matters of particular theological importance for which time can hardly be found in the General Synod's overcrowded agendas. The other machinery of Church government has been similarly streamlined, the old diocesan and ruridecanal conferences being replaced by smaller synods, which inevitably have to deal with much the same matters as before, with financial affairs still occupying the predominant place.

Experiments in Worship

But if as a whole the changes in Church government made

comparatively little impact at parochial level, the introductions of experiments in worship most certainly did. Of these, the new services of Holy Communion caused the greatest interest. For some years, increasing stress had been laid in many parishes on making the Parish Communion the main act of worship each Sunday morning, and relegating Morning Prayer to be said or sung afterwards for the few elderly members of the congregation who valued its continuation. The numerous translations of the Bible into modern English, culminating in the *New English Bible* which appeared in 1970 (the New Testament alone in 1961) had accustomed worshippers to such readings in church; thereafter it was a small step to using prayers in more modern language. The introduction of what were called Series II and Series III brought first conservative alterations, and later those of a more radical kind to sacramental worship. (Series I was a virtual re-issue of the service of 1549.) Series II was widely welcomed, and proved a unifying factor in churches which had previously practised a variety of usages. Series III introduced the modern pronouns instead of the traditional "thee" and "thou", but once the shock of addressing the Deity as "You" had been overcome, the content of the new service and its structure were a help to many, especially to young people. Individual parish clergy found varying degrees of support for these alterations, but within a few years, a large number of parishes of all shades of churchmanship had opted for Series II, with the newer Series III gaining increasing acceptance, at least one cathedral adopting it for its main morning worship, with full choral accompaniment.

Durford, under a new incumbent, Leslie Marriott, proceeded with little persuasion from "1662" to Series II and III, but Monksland experimented with Series I, and had some difficulty in introducing Series III once a month. This pleased nobody, and Basil Pearson sometimes found himself obliged to exercise a calming effect as chairman, when feelings ran high at his parochial church council meetings. The new baptismal service brought a less enthusiastic response, and though held on a number of occasions, both incumbents found parents asking that the 1662 Prayer Book service might be used for the baptism of their children.

The Mass Media and Commercial Techniques

Meanwhile the enormous impact made on the country after the war by television became visible through the sprouting of aerials from almost every house in town and village within a few years. The Church endeavoured to come to terms with the new medium by televising church services, and occasional plays, but found difficulty in making the best use of this valuable new medium of communication, largely through lack of financial resources. Religious broadcasting experts noted that greater public response came from radio than from television programmes, indicating the continuing importance of the spoken word as compared with films and drama. Two fields of communication, however, showed notable advances. The founding of the College of Preachers in 1960 brought some twenty clergy together in each course, lasting for the inside of a week, and held in different parts of the country. Lectures on preaching content and techniques, together with advice on mannerisms and the use of the voice, sent many men back to their parishes with a new determination to improve their sermons in clarity, interest, and method of construction. Well over a thousand of the clergy have so far participated in such courses, which have received general support from the bishops. At the same time, a series of courses for many categories of clergy was begun in the 1960's at St. George's House, Windsor, to provide further opportunities for a deepening understanding of methods of business management and industrial problems, while courses to help those engaged in urban ministry have also been arranged in various other centres. All this has resulted in the realisation that study in depth of modern methods of communication and commercial techniques can be of great advantage to such clergymen able to profit from these opportunities of in-service training.

The Ordination of Women

A further development in ministry has resulted from a falling off in numbers of those offering themselves for ordination. Older men have been accepted for non-residential training by attending evening courses extended over several years in order to be ordained to what is called the auxiliary pastoral ministry. Before ordination, these men must be sponsored not only by their bishops, but by the incumbents and church councils of their home parishes. This project has caused some debate; will these men, it is asked, be a kind of second-class priesthood? Others feel that with a general shortage of clergy, many smaller parishes, especially in rural areas, will still be able to retain a resident incumbent which would otherwise be impossible. A more controversial subject has been the pressure by some for the ordination of women to the priesthood. A single case in the diocese of Hong Kong was pronounced "ultra vires" by Archbishop William Temple during the war years. Since then, several such ordinations have taken place in the Episcopal Church in America, but these have been regarded with general disfavour elsewhere in the Anglican Communion. Such a momentous step, it is felt, must be taken with a full measure of consent, and with due regard for its consequences in ecumenical relations.

The Church: more lively but more vulnerable

With a quarter of the twentieth century still remaining, Basil Pearson and Leslie Marriott find themselves faced with many problems, spiritual, social, and financial. The sheer pressures of life bear heavily on them and their families as they struggle against indifference on the part of the vast majority. Growing signs of more definite opposition, moreover, indicate the possibility of increased hostility through violence and the attractions of the occult. Monksland church became the victim of dark practices, and churchyard monuments were disturbed. Late in 1974, Archbishop Ramsey retired from the archbishopric of Canterbury. His last act was to see the passing into law of the General Synod's resolution to be itself the final authority in deciding all matters of doctrine and worship in the Church of England. When asked what were the chief differences since he took office in 1961, he replied: "I find the Church today less secure, more vulnerable and more lively". If this is indeed the case, we may hope that the Holy Spirit's life-giving power will bring greater energy and a more steadfast faith to the clergy and people of Britain in the years that lie ahead.